Essentials of Online Course Design

In spite of the proliferation of online learning in higher education, creating online courses can still evoke a good deal of frustration, negativity, and wariness in those who need to create them.

Essentials of Online Course Design: A Standards-Based Guide takes a fresh, thoughtfully designed, step-by-step approach to online course development. At its core is a set of standards that are based on best practices in the field of online teaching and learning. Pedagogical, organizational, and visual design principles are presented and modeled throughout the book, and users will quickly learn from the guide's hands-on approach. The course design process begins with the elements of a classroom syllabus, which, after a series of guided steps, easily evolve into an online course outline.

The guide's key features include:

- A practical approach informed by theory.
- Clean interior design that offers straightforward guidance from page 1.
- Clear and jargon-free language.
- Examples, screenshots, and illustrations to clarify and support the text.
- A companion website with examples, adaptable templates, interactive learning features, and online resources.
- A checklist of online course design standards that readers can use to self-evaluate.

Essentials of Online Course Design: A Standards-Based Guide serves as a best-practices model for designing online courses. After reading this book, readers will find that preparing for online teaching is, contrary to popular belief, a satisfying and engaging experience. The core issue is simply good design: pedagogical, organizational, and visual.

Marjorie Vai has been directly involved with online education and training for almost 25 years. Most recently, she designed and developed the online Masters Degree Program in Teaching English to Speakers of Other Languages (MATESOL) at The New School, New York.

Kristen Sosulski is the Academic Director of Distance Learning and a Clinical Assistant Professor at New York University's School of Continuing and Professional Studies.

A special dedication from Marjorie to Susan Kinsey who has been a good, wise, and supportive friend. Her belief in my vision for this book has been a constant source of comfort.

We both want to dedicate the work we've done in putting this book and website together to online teachers everywhere.

Essentials of Online Course Design

A Standards-Based Guide

Marjorie Vai and
Kristen Sosulski

Routledge
Taylor & Francis Group

NEW YORK AND LONDON

First published 2011
by Routledge
270 Madison Avenue, New York, NY 10016

Simultaneously published in the UK
by Routledge
2 Park Square, Milton Park, Abingdon, Oxon OX14 4RN

Routledge is an imprint of the Taylor & Francis Group, an informa business

© 2011 Taylor & Francis

The right of Marjorie Vai and Kristen Sosulski to be identified as authors of this work has been asserted by them in accordance with sections 77 and 78 of the Copyright, Designs and Patents Act 1988.

Typeset in Helvetica Neue and Optima by
Florence Production Ltd, Stoodleigh, Devon

Printed and bound in the United States of America
on acid-free paper by
Edwards Brothers, Inc.

Library of Congress Cataloging in Publication Data
Vai, Marjorie.
   The essential guide to online course design: a standards based guide / by Marjorie Vai & Kristen Sosulski.
      p. cm.
    1. Web-based instruction—Design—Handbooks, manuals, etc.
   2. Web-based instruction—Design—Standards—Handbooks, manuals, etc.   3. Instructional systems—Design—Handbooks, manuals, etc.
   4. Instructional systems—Design—Standards—Handbooks, manuals, etc.   I. Sosulski, Kristen. II. Title.
   LB1044.87.V35 2011
   378.1'25—dc22   2010031442

ISBN13: 978-0-415-87299-7 (hbk)
ISBN13: 978-0-415-87300-0 (pbk)
ISBN13: 978-0-203-83831-0 (ebk)

Contents

Foreword

When I pick up a new book in my fields of language education and technology-mediated learning, I am sometimes struck by bad thoughts.

If the book is really good, I wish that I had written it, and I had thought of this new approach to teaching and learning. Thankfully rare are the books that engender such wicked thoughts.

But this is one of those books.

Essentials of Online Course Design explains how to design, build, and implement online learning solutions, to ensure that learners receive high quality educational engagement. The book aims to meet the needs of different groups of readers and practitioners who are anxious to learn more about the design of successful online learning courses—and what makes them successful.

As an experienced geek myself, and having spent many years melding the technical and the pedagogical, I have bought many books and attended many courses that purported to explain how online learning worked, and how I should design a course.

In many cases these offered me technical solutions while ignoring the pedagogical issues. Others gave me pedagogical theory but no support in implementing it in a way that learners could enjoy. Few of them focused on the impact that visual design and user experience design would have on the learning process.

That is why this book is so important. I know of no other book that combines a focus on pedagogical learning design and all that entails, with technical background and support, with expert insights into the world of visual design and optimising the user experience. This provides an added dimension for the online course designer—the melding of key standards of course design but seen from new angles and with added depth and breadth.

The book aims, as the authors state in the Preface, to "model simple and intelligent design and provide abundant examples of good online design." Throughout the book this is exactly what they do.

One of the beauties of this book is that it can be read and utilised practically and successfully by a wide range of education professionals, not all of whom are geeks or Blackboard experts or devotees of Moodle (or even know what that is).

It is aimed at a broader, non-technical readership and yet maintains an intellectual discipline that demands much of its readership.

The focus on the practitioner shines through from every page— the inclusion of personal statements from practitioners about how they have learned and taught, along with screenshots and real-world examples of course design in action, help the teacher internalize the skills and competences needed for successful design.

The book offers practical advice which is, in the words of the authors, "informed by theory but not about theory"—precisely what a professional practitioner needs. It also offers a supporting website where practitioners can find further guidance and resources such as templates.

The book helps teachers move, in Argyris and Schon's terms, from "espoused theory" to "theory in use"—from what we say we believe we should do, to what we actually do.

The authors are uniquely qualified to produce this book. Marjorie Vai has been an innovator in language teaching for many years, and has always been a leader in the application of technology to learning. She published innovative software solutions for language learning long before most publishers and teachers had begun to appreciate the benefits to the learner of a technology-mediated learning resource. Marjorie has designed and implemented a ground-breaking online Masters program in TESOL for the New School in New York (full disclosure: I wrote one of the modules) and launched a new style of learning (and opened new channels of access to that learning) for TESOL professionals globally.

Kristen Sosulski has a solid grounding in online theory and practice, and oversees the online program in one of the most respected universities in the U.S.

For me a crucial focus of the book is how to engage the learner. This is the basis of constructivist learning theory—that learning must be an active process—and at the heart of every successful teacher or trainer's toolkit. Teachers must know how to engage learners, to motivate, involve, and guide them to learning success.

I hope this book helps teachers and course designers worldwide achieve more for their learners and clients. I am certain it will support the raising of standards in online learning across multiple disciplines and academic fields.

Michael Carrier
Head of English Language Innovation
British Council, London

Preface

Marjorie Vai: John Maeda wrote his small book *The Laws of Simplicity* (2006) to address the need for simple solutions when dealing with the complexities of our technologically-oriented world. For Maeda, this became a personal mission, and was a focus of his research at MIT.

Maeda inspires the approach we take in the design of this project. "For the foreseeable future, complicated technologies will continue to invade our homes and workplaces, thus simplicity is bound to be a growth industry."

Consumers can usually find an array of easy-to-follow books on computers and technology. Educators have not been so lucky. Simplicity of design helps cut through the technological mire and saves time. It opens the mind and pleases the eye.

This guide models simple and intelligent design, and provides abundant examples of good online course design. And so, we will reference both Maeda and other designers, along with academic specialists.

Most of my professional life has been spent working in publishing and academia in the field of teaching English (TESOL) as educator, publisher, author, and administrator. For 20 years, I served as founding director and then chair of the English Language Studies department at The New School in New York City. I designed and developed several programs both onsite and online, including an internationally-oriented online Masters Degree Program in Teaching English to Speakers of Other Languages (MATESOL). Students and teachers were involved from around the world.

When the time came to train the MATESOL faculty in online course development, what we needed was a book for each teacher that first explained how online worked, then modeled and walked instructors through the process of developing a well-designed online course. Such a book would, I assumed, focus on standards of good design.

There were theoretical books. There were books that seemed to be written by people in the field of educational technology for other people in educational technology. Other books outlined a process but offered no examples of good course design (as though an understanding of good online design were intuitive). There were whole books on single aspects of course design (working collaboratively, creating activities, etc.). Some referenced some standards of good design but were not comprehensive. Creating our own comprehensive set of materials at The New School was unrealistic.

The bottom line: there was no guide that you could give an instructor that simply and intelligently walked them through the online course design process. And certainly there was no approach organized and modeled on standards or best practices for online education. This was the case, in spite of the proliferation of online education around the world. So, I became intent on developing such a guide; a guide that has now evolved into a larger project including a supporting website full of resources.

My own experience working with online media began about 25 years ago as a writer and contributing editor for *Dowline*, the magazine of Dow Jones Online Services. It was there that I developed the habit of paying careful attention to all aspects of instructional design—pedagogical, organizational, and visual.

Teachers need simple, straightforward guidance on how to use technology so that subject matter is the central focus of their efforts. Students need engaging and easy-to-use learning environments. This guide is hands-on and practical. It is informed by theory, but not about theory. It addresses the practical task at hand—designing an online course, based on a set of accepted standards.

I was confident that I could write this guide. However, what I needed was a co-author with long-term experience working with the kinds of instructors who need books like this.

Fortunately, I met and got to know Kristen Sosulski, Academic Director at the Office of Distance Learning at New York University. Kristen shared my focus and vision for the project. She brings to this project both a strong background in theory and a first-hand understanding of the realistic needs of online instructors and learners.

http://www.marjorievai.com

Kristen Sosulski: Throughout my career as an educator, I have collaborated with university faculty to explore the ways in which technology can be used to facilitate and enhance teaching and learning. At the New York University Office of Distance Learning, I lead a team that partners with faculty to develop high-quality online courses. I've found that, in addition to the support we provide, faculty members continually request a simple guide to walk them through the process of transforming their traditional classroom courses into online courses. Simply put, there is a lot for teachers to learn when embarking on the creation of their first online course. There are pedagogical, organizational, technical, and administrative considerations to keep in mind. With time and resources always at a minimum, it can be challenging to demonstrate best practices while simultaneously guiding teachers through the "how to" of teaching online.

When Marjorie asked me to co-author this book, I was delighted. I knew how important a simple guide to online course design was to our own faculty, here and abroad. I also knew from conferences and colleagues in the field that this seemed to be true across the board. Marjorie's vision for a simple, concise, and clearly written guide to online course design encouraged me to reflect on my own work with faculty and, in the process, to develop new ways to mentor them.

Whether you are a new or seasoned online teacher, this guide will serve your professional needs well by providing you with a streamlined set of organizational, pedagogical, and visual-design standards, which can serve as the foundation for any online course. The standards checklist alone is an invaluable resource and is intended to serve as a reminder for all course developers.

This is a great guide for students in educational technology programs who are learning about instructional design principles. The book exemplifies many of the best practices in the field. The examples we provide from featured teachers show how they are applied in an authentic setting.

One major challenge all teachers face is how to ensure that their students remain engaged throughout their courses. Chapters 5–8 provide excellent examples of lessons, resources, activities, and appropriate assessments for use in online courses. I am particularly excited by the activity types that we put together, and our website, which supplements this book by providing models and examples.

In my experience, teachers need guidance in developing digitally-based materials for their online courses. Considerations such as writing style, layout, and use of media tend to be overlooked. This book highlights the importance of these design elements through concrete examples and guidelines.

One of the most difficult concepts to translate to the online medium is that of time. Chapter 1 visually illustrates how to structure time in an online course and Chapter 9 helps teachers design online syllabi to reflect a timeline that is appropriate for an online course.

Together, we present this simple guide to online course design. I would like to thank Marjorie for inviting me to work with her to create this essential resource for teachers, support staff working with teachers, and trainers to guide them through the online course design process.

Acknowledgments

This book could not have been everything we envisioned without the full cooperation of our publisher, Routledge. *Essentials of Online Course Design: A Standards-Based Guide* exemplifies as many standards of online course design as a book can. We firstly want to thank our current editor, Alex Masulis. He has been very supportive and successfully communicated the importance of the design features to the production department in the UK. We would like to acknowledge all involved with the production of the book with special thanks to Sarah Stone, Sue Leaper, Charlotte Hiorns and Andrew Craddock for their fine work in following through on our design, and editorial concerns.

We are also grateful to Sarah Burrows, former editor at Routledge, for recognizing the value of our vision and for initially supporting the project.

The fine work of featured teachers Joelle Scally and Scott Thornbury enabled us to provide our readers with real world examples and voices. Their contributions have added much to the practical, hands-on quality of the book.

We appreciate the ability to use and feature two LMSs, Epsilen and E360, in portions of the book.

Finally, we want to thank Steve Goss, Kristen's husband, for the elegant design he created for the cover of the book. It evokes those central ideas of simplicity, clarity, engagement, interactivity, and collaboration that are emphasized throughout the text.

Marjorie Vai: First and foremost, I am very grateful to my co-author, Kristen Sosulski, for her excellent contribution to this book. It has been a pleasure working with her and getting to know her. She is a fine person as well as as a fine co-author.

Acknowledgments

My views about what is important for successful online study owe much to The New School pioneers who started the online learning program there in 1994. They were (with titles from then): Elizabeth Dickey, Dean of The New School; Stephen Anspacher, founding Director of the online program; and Elissa Tenny, Associate Dean. They emphasized training online teachers, standards of good course design, and a general can-do attitude that encouraged department heads and imaginative teachers to develop quality online courses and programs. I also need to acknowledge Dhal Anglada, the gifted instructional designer who worked with me during the design phase of the online MATESOL at The New School.

My early experience writing for Dow Jones Online Services was critical in developing my thinking on online engagement and accessibility. I thank Cathy Smith my editor at Dow Jones, for her role in encouraging my work and constantly presenting me with new challenges.

As for family and friends, I want to thank Lynne, Robyn, Daniel, and Michael for their support.

Kristen Sosulski: First, I would like to begin by thanking my colleague, best friend, and husband, Steven Goss, Director of Online Education, Bank Street College. He's been my number one advocate. He has been extremely generous in providing thoughtful feedback and examples for this book.

I'm so grateful to Susan Kinsey, Divisional Dean, NYU-SCPS who introduced Marjorie and me. Without her, Marjorie and I would not have co-authored this book and become good friends in the process. I want to especially thank Marjorie, for her friendship, inspiration, and giving me the opportunity to reflect on my practice by working on this book.

I would like to express my gratitude to Robert Lapiner, Dean, NYU-SCPS, for his enthusiasm and confidence in me. He's been a champion for me and my work and a huge supporter for online education. Also, a special thanks to Dennis DiLorenzo, Associate Dean NYU-SCPS who has given me the tools and resources to build a successful online learning team.

A very special thanks to the NYU SCPS Distance Learning team (Ted Bongiovanni, Vanessa Carrion, Bancha Srikacha, Vladimir Merisca, Bobby Aviles, and Mary Ann Mazzella) and all the NYU faculty and students who gave me the opportunity to collaborate and grow with them. Some of them are featured in this book.

Deep appreciation is extended to Robert Manuel, Dean of the School of Continuing Studies, Georgetown University. He gave me the opportunity to teach my first online course, and was gracious enough to provide me with thoughtful feedback on this book.

Also, it's been an honor to have Felice Nudelman, Executive Director of Education at *The New York Times* provide feedback on this book.

Finally, I'd like to thank my parents, Deborah and Richard Sosulski for encouragement and ongoing support while I was writing this book.

Order and simplification
are the first steps towards the
mastery of a subject.

Thomas Mann

Introduction to this Guide

How simple can you make it? ⟷ How complex does it have to be?

Source: Maeda (2006)

To design is much more than simply to assemble, to order, or even to edit; it is to add value and meaning, to illuminate, to simplify, to clarify, to modify, to dignify, to dramatize, to persuade, and perhaps even to amuse.

Paul Rand—author, graphic designer, teacher

To borrow some words from Paul Rand above, this guide aims to simplify, to clarify, and to illuminate. We hope you find that it helps you to do the same in your online course.

i.1 A Unique Guide for Online Course Design

This is the only book on this topic that has all these qualities:

- A clearly outlined set of **online course design standards** establishes the core principles.

- The **guide itself serves as a model** of many of the design elements espoused.

- The step-by-step development process builds the online course up **from syllabus to course framework to final course**.

- The writing is **concise and clear**, and avoids jargon.

- The content focuses on **practical application informed by theory**.

- Examples and illustrations of good online course design are provided throughout the book and on the book's website.

- The book's website, www.routledge.com/textbooks/ 9780415873000, provides additional reference and resource materials, templates for units, and models of good online course design. Look for the website icon throughout the book.

- A standards checklist enables readers to do a reflective self-evaluation of the work they have done.

- Learning styles are emphasized and modeled in examples, and in the way the guide itself is written and designed.

i.2 Who Is the Guide and Website For?

The guide and website are for those involved with online teaching and training at all levels, including:

- Higher education teachers who face the short- or long-term realities of transforming an onsite course to online.

- Staff development trainers who work through the online course-building process with teachers.

- High-school teachers developing online courses.

- Instructors teaching courses on online course design in schools of education (i.e. educational technology programs). The standards-based models and examples reduce the burden on these instructors to provide such resources on their own.

- Students in educational technology programs who will be working in the field or taking a course in the area.

- Trainers to those learning about online pedagogical design. Again, the standards-based models support the process.

- Higher-level administrators who need to understand the elements of good online course design.

- Individuals within an institution, or entrepreneurs who wish to initiate online course development or training. Given the availability of learning management systems such as Moodle, anyone can begin an educational or training program, provided they have the ability to do so and a market for their offerings.

- Anyone interested in learning about, or brushing up on, best practices in teaching with technologies.

i.3 What Do Online Students Need?

After years of traditional classroom study, most students have questions about studying online. For those committing to more than one course (e.g. a program or degree), they may have even more questions. Some examples:

- What is it like taking a course online?

- How does online work?

- How does it compare to classroom study?

- Does it require special technical knowledge?

- Can I get help if I have technical problems?

- Will studying at a computer be boring?

- Will there be help if I find I have problems with online study?

- Will I feel isolated studying online? Will I miss out on working within a community?

- How much of my time will an online course require compared to taking an onsite course?

- How do you do hands-on in an online environment?

Of course, you can always find answers that will satisfy students enough to get them to sign up for the course. However, there are still academic programs that post long lectures (in type, video, or audio) in online courses. They may submit students and teachers to painfully long encounters with discussion boards or emails. Some students who have made the commitment may stick with it in spite of these issues, and some not.

Online programs at even some of the best universities have been poorly designed or ill-conceived. Sometimes students feel that they are adrift without support or a sense of structure or community. Instructors may feel the same. Good, well-intentioned universities have had programs that have crashed and burned because they couldn't create courses that consistently engaged and challenged. How can this be avoided?

Instructors and teachers should be able to answer the questions outlined above so that students feel confident about the process and its benefits. This book provides the answers and the means of following through on promises made. Standards of good online design are at the core of this process.

i.4   A Standards-Based Approach

A great deal of work and research has been done to determine what works in an online learning and teaching environment. As a result, standards and best practices have been developed to guide course designers and teachers. Often such standards are presented in complicated or dense formats. We have tried to simplify the process of applying standards in this guide so that you will have more time to spend on the challenging task of rethinking your content for online study.

Essentials of Online Course Design; A Standards-Based Guide takes a carefully designed, step-by-step approach to creating an online course. At its core, the standards are reinforced in a variety of ways and finally presented as a checklist that teachers can use to reflectively self-evaluate their online course.

We present standards in three stages:

1. In each chapter as they are covered. At this stage they look like this:

   ☑ Presentations of new knowledge and skills, activities, and assessments address a variety of learning styles.

2. Next, all standards covered in a chapter are listed in summary form at the end of the chapter. Use this to review the points covered in the chapter, or as a focused checklist when working through the chapter topic in your course. At this stage the squares in front of the standards are open— waiting for you to check them.

> ☐ **Presentations of new knowledge and skills, activities, and assessments address a variety of learning styles.**

3. Finally, Appendix B is a standards checklist for you to use when you have developed your course. This also serves as a standards index so that you can go back to the points where the standard was covered, and review where and how each was presented. Each standard is followed by the page numbers where it comes up so that you can review as needed.

The redundancy built into this small guide reinforces your understanding of the essentials of good online design.

Underlying Principles

These standards have been culled from a number of resources and our own experiences of creating and developing online courses and multimedia projects. They are presented and reinforced in a straightforward and constructive way. Some of the major resources we have used are:

- Chickering, A.W. & Gamson, Z.F. (1987) "Seven Principles for Good Practice in Undergraduate Education," *The American Association for Higher Education Bulletin*, March.

- Horton, S. (2006) "Design Simply. Universal Usability: A Universal Design Approach to Web Usability," available at www.universalusability.com (accessed April 21, 2010).

- Lidwell, W., Holden, K., & Butler, J. (2003) *Universal Principles of Design: 125 Ways to Influence Perception, Increase Appeal, Make Better Design Decisions, and Teach Through Design*, Beverly, MA: Rockport Publishers.

- Lynch, P.J. & Horton, S. (2009) *Web Style Guide*, 3rd Edition, New Haven, CT: Yale University Press, available at http://webstyleguide.com (accessed May 3, 2010).

- Maeda, J. (2006) *Laws of Simplicity*, Cambridge, MA: MIT Press.

- Mayer, R.E. (2001) *Multimedia Learning*, New York: Cambridge University Press.

- Palloff, R.M. & Pratt, K. (2007) *Building Online Learning Communities*, San Francisco, CA: Jossey-Bass.

- Quality Matters (2006) "Inter-institutional Quality Assurance in Online Learning," available at www.qualitymatters.org.

Note: A full list of sources and references can be found on pages 196–197.

i.5 Organization of the Book

The book is organized as follows:

- The **Introduction** provides an overview of the book, with time spent on basic issues including notes on the terminology used in the book, and a brief description of the website and how it relates to the book.

- Chapter 1, **Orientation to Online Teaching and Learning**, introduces aspects of and priorities for online teaching and learning that may be new to you.

- Chapter 2, **Elements of an Online Course**, is an illustrated tour through the elements of a learning management system (LMS), using real examples from an online course.

- Chapters 3 and 4, **Language and Writing Style** and **Visual Design Basics**, cover two core aspects that are not unique to online. Teachers must be aware of the critical importance of adapting these to online.

- Chapters 5, 6, 7, and 8, **Engaging the Online Learner**, **Activities and Tools**, **Resources that Engage**, and

Assessment and Feedback, cover the essential elements of the presentation and design of the course, such as introducing new knowledge, activities, resources, and assessment.

- Chapters 9 and 10, **Building the Course Foundation** and **Creating the Course Structure**, begin by using the standard elements of a classroom syllabus as a point of departure to create an online syllabus. After a series of guided steps, this evolves into the online course framework as presented in Chapter 10.

- Appendix A, **Writing Learning Outcomes**, reviews the essential points of writing good learning outcomes.

- Appendix B, **The Standards Checklist**, summarizes the standards in a checklist format.

The accompanying website provides many models of good online design, and additional references and resources. Adaptable templates help readers to conceptualize and develop the substance of each learning unit. Again, all concepts and elements in this guide are reinforced through models and examples that emphasize online course design standards. It also covers multimedia basics for making your own material.

i.6 How to Use the Guide

If you have the time, we suggest that you review everything and look at the examples. This can only strengthen your basic understanding of the online design process so that, later, you can focus on your content.

However, depending upon your time frame and/or what you may already know, you may find one or more topics that you can bypass. If writing learning outcomes is second nature to you, for example, you can skip that section. If you have taken online courses and are familiar with time considerations and learning management systems, you may want to skip those sections.

A great deal of time and space in this project has been devoted to assembling the models and examples of good course design that appear in the book and on the website. Familiarizing yourself with these examples will strengthen your skills in online course design.

The organization of the website mirrors that of the book. So if, for example, you are guided to web materials in Section 9.2 of the book, you will find them in Section 9.2 on the website.

i.7 This Guide as a Model

Standards are modeled in the way this guide is written and designed. The modeling in the guide, of course, is limited to the qualities a book and an online course share. Flip through the pages and notice what has been done in the following categories:

Graphic Design

- This is an easily readable typeface.

- Right margins are jagged.

- There is ample space between the lines of text.

- The pages are uncluttered.

- There is a good deal of white space on the page—there is no crowding.

- Bold type is used sparingly for emphasis.

- Graphic design elements are used consistently.

Images, Audio, and Video

- Visual elements are used to improve clarity of presentation and understanding—they enhance rather than distract from learning.

- All elements in images are easily discernible.

- A variety of visual and text elements support different styles of learning.

Language and Writing Style

- Language is clear, brief, and to the point.

- The tone is relaxed, conversational, and supportive.

- Jargon and technical terms are avoided whenever possible, or defined.

- Bullets are used for lists, and numbers are used for sequenced items.

Learning Resources

- An ample number of models and examples are presented.

- A rich collection of links and references to online resources, books, and articles are included in the book and on the website.

- A full list of references is included at the back of the book.

Chapter Structure

- An introduction begins the chapter.

- "Chunking" (i.e. breaking down content into smaller sections than you might normally find in a book) is used to reflect the breakdown needed when material is presented online.

- Practical resources are included for exploration and expansion of the topic.

- The chapter ends with a list of standards that serves as a summary of core points.

Real-world Examples

The website is a rich source of additional resources, such as:

- full-color screenshots

- examples of lessons and activities

- downloadable templates

- videos, and

- additional references.

i.8   Terminology in this Guide

For the sake of consistency, we have used specific words or phrases to represent, in some cases, a variety of possibilities. Once again, we have also done this for the sake of simplicity.

Units
Lessons
Sections
Segments

Unit structure

- **Teacher**. The course designer/developer, instructor, professor, facilitator, or trainer. While phrases such as teacher and facilitator may suggest two approaches that are fairly far apart, this guide does not cover the actual running of the course and therefore tries to take as neutral a position as possible. Whether we are talking about the teacher or the designer/developer will be made clear from the context.

- **Student**. The individual that is taking the online course (i.e. the trainee, class member, or participant).

- **Learner**. This term is used when we refer to the ways an individual obtains knowledge.

- **Course**. We use this term to cover any of the following: university or college course, high-school class, training program, seminar, or workshop.

- **Lesson**. A unit of instruction that distinguishes the different topics within an online course, which the learners cover in a particular order. You will see, even in this guide, that there are many different terms used in different ways to divide things up. There is, especially, a great deal of variety on the lesson level. It can also be called: module, lecture, or section.

- **Learning management system (LMS)**. The LMS is the web-based software application used to design, develop, teach, and manage online courses. It is ultimately the virtual environment in which the learner engages with the content, peers, and teacher. It is sometimes called a course management system (CMS).

- **Onsite course**. A course that is taught in a physical location where teachers and learners are present in a face-to-face setting.

- **Gender**. We simply use both male and female in our examples and writing.

Chapter 1 Orientation to Online Teaching and Learning

Learn—Knowledge makes everything simpler.

Maeda (2006), 4th law of simplicity

In this chapter we look at some of the key characteristics of teaching online. Some, such as format and delivery, are unique to teaching online. Others, such as how time is used, the structure of an online class, and communicating without face-to-face contact require understanding and some adaptation.

Make no mistake about it—your first experience teaching online will require adjustments. The following will most certainly be different from teaching onsite:

- **Absence of a physical teaching space**. You no longer have a brick and mortar classroom! This completely changes the way you interact with your students. For example, assignment instructions are usually written and lectures must be re-conceived for the online environment.

- **Planning and creating online class content**. Ideally, all or most of this happens before the class begins. This guide walks you through the process.

- **Communicating online rather than in person**. Whatever non-verbal communication techniques you use in class will now be replaced with something else—the tone of your writing, written encouragement, and perhaps some audio or video so that learners can associate your personality with the written text. On a one-on-one level, you will be in contact through emails or by phone.

- **Delayed feedback**. You won't be there to clarify points as needed. So, it becomes important to use a writing style that is clear and straightforward. At times you will clarify by using references to online resources or definitions. Also, it is important to anticipate questions from students ahead of time and articulate the answers within your instructions for activities, assignments, etc.

- **Visual design**. Simple, organized, and clean page design supports clarity and understanding. Using images, and restating or providing examples in audio or video may help as well.

- **Flexibility**. When you add flexibility, you lose a certain amount of structure. Deadlines now play a key role in providing structure.

- **Time online**. You and the learners will need to adjust to how your time is used. We cover this in detail below.

- **Class participation vs. attending class**. The quantity and quality of online class participation replaces onsite attendance.

- **Office hours**. The way you provide extra help to students and answer questions will change, somewhat. Setting up office hours by phone or text/video/audio chat (e.g. Skype and Google Chat) are possible. Note: This doesn't always work with international learners because of the time differences. However, scheduling one-on-one phone or real-time chat meetings with individuals is often possible.

1.1 Online Learning in the Twenty-First Century

> Students who took all or part of their class online performed better, on average, than those taking the same course through traditional face-to-face instruction.
>
> U.S. Department of Education (2009)

According to Marc Prensky, today's learners are not the people our educational system was designed to teach:

> It is now clear that as a result of this ubiquitous (digital) environment and the sheer volume of their interaction with it, today's learners think and process information fundamentally differently from their predecessors... we can say with certainty that their thinking patterns have changed... Our learners today are all "native speakers" of the digital language of computers, video games and the Internet.
>
> Prensky (2001)

In many parts of the world, learners that were 25 or younger at the publication of this book have probably grown up with computers, video games, word processing, and the internet. They have easy, portable access to the music, art, and entertainment of their liking, as well as at-their-fingertips access to large numbers of people that share their interests or have information they want.

These learners are not the passive recipients of such technology, as their parents might have been. They can and most often prefer to be players in multi-user environments. They use their imagination and creativity freely and openly. They work, play, and compete with people around the globe. These learners are used to levels of engagement, collaboration, interactivity, access, and instant feedback that could not be imagined 25 years ago.

And what of the older learners and teachers among us, the "digital immigrants" who were not brought up using the technology, but want to or have to embrace it now? We must adapt. And why not, it's pretty exciting stuff.

We can begin here by becoming familiar with the elements and standards that make for a good online course. Visual, pedagogical, and organizational design needs to be clear and engaging enough for all to get it, "natives" and "immigrants" alike.

This guide introduces the pedagogical essentials of twenty-first-century online course design.

1.2 Asynchronous Learning

Real time is another term that can be used for **synchronous**.

Synchronous means that things are happening at the same time. **Asynchronous means that things are happening at different times.**

If a teacher in New York is teaching an onsite class, or if an online class is being taught in real time, it is happening in a synchronous time frame. Teacher and learners are communicating within the same time frame.

Reflection

Who Are Your Learners?

We can't generalize about who your learners will be. Let's look at some characteristics of online learners.

Many of your learners will fall under more than one category below. Many of you will have a variety of different students. We hope that this helps you to put yourself in their place and imagine what it's like to be an online student. We also suggest that you take an online course if you have the opportunity, the time, and haven't done so already.

- The "digital pros" are 25 or under. They grew up using the internet and email. They are used to scanning web pages, reading short messages on email, text messaging, and using social media websites such as Twitter and Facebook. Digital pros can't conceive of a life without digital media.
- The "digitally evolved" Gen Xers grew up with computers but typically were introduced to the internet in high school or college. They may or may not find using digital/social media second nature, depending upon their background and attitude.
- The "digital adopters" use computers but are used to reading longer texts, papers, and magazines. They are fairly comfortable with doing the basics on a computer, but may not feel comfortable jumping into a totally digital world with lots of bells and whistles.
- The pre-digital learners may be taking an online class simply because there is no other choice. They know little about computers.
- International learners' first language is not English. They rely on the fact that the teacher is sensitive to this without being patronizing. Many of you who use this book will have entire classes of learners whose native language is something other than English. The chances are there will be some variation in cultures and first languages in most online classes.
- The classic (young) learners are probably also digital pros. They may be in high school, a community college, or a 4-year college. They may still be in the process of developing a writing style. Some may have trouble with grammar structure and use.
- Adult (probably working) learners have neither time nor money to waste. They may or may not be comfortable with the digital world. This group may or may not have difficulties with their writing, and the structure and use of grammar.

Look over this list again. Which of these groups do you belong in? Focus especially on those that are different from you and try to put yourself in their place.

This book focuses on asynchronous learning. This is how it works: the teacher may post material online at 9 a.m. on Monday in Toronto. Learners, who may be situated anywhere in the world, can access that material and respond any time, night or day, within a defined number of days.

Asynchronous learning is more flexible than real-time learning since the class is not fixed at a set time period. Consequently, it is preferred by learners with busy lives, complicated schedules, or burdensome commutes. Learners can participate at a time of day that is convenient. The same, of course, is true for the teacher.

An asynchronous online course follows the daily personal schedule of learner and teacher. Class meets at no particular time and is of no specific length. In fact, an online class doesn't actually meet in the sense that it does onsite. The learners do not need to be online together at any particular time.

Asynchronous online study is really the only convenient possibility for international or global study because of the time differences. It is also an ideal setup for people who travel a lot since they can teach and/or learn on the go.

Asynchronous learning allows for flexibility of:

- **Time**. One can study any time, day or night, within a series of fixed time periods.

- **Place**. To access the course one need only be able to access the internet. Parts of a well-designed course are portable (i.e. downloadable for viewing, printing, listening, or watching when you are offline). Given the proliferation of smartphones such as the iPhone, or devices such as the iPad or other electronic readers, learners can study on the go.

- **Pace**. Learners move through the course at their own pace—up to a point. They move more quickly through areas they know, or that are easy for them. They treat more difficult subjects more deliberately. For added support, they can easily research points within the course using the internet. These possibilities offer learners additional sources of support (once they know about them).

- **Participation**. There is no pressure on learners to respond to comments and questions immediately as there is for an onsite course. The ability to reflect before responding is one of the benefits of online learning and should be encouraged. Once learners have taken other learners' comments into consideration, they may want to or have to (depending on the teacher's specified requirements) respond again. They sense that they are contributing to a knowledge base—bringing in related materials, reconsidering issues, reconstituting the class in a way. This naturally becomes a learner-centered environment. It facilitates the development of higher-level thinking skills. Evaluation and re-evaluation become a core part of the learning process.

In addition to asynchronous and synchronous online formats, there is a third type of format: **blended learning**. This is any combination of at least two of the following: asynchronous online, real-time (synchronous) online, or onsite learning. Synchronous activities can be a good complement to an asynchronous course, circumstances permitting.

1.3 Online Course Delivery

A learning management system (LMS) can be, and usually is, the program used to create and manage an online course. LMSs such as Moodle or Blackboard (see Figure 1.1) do not require that you be a "techno-wizard." However, computer literacy is a must. You need to know how to use some of the most basic programs such as a word processor, spreadsheet, photo manager, and email. Understanding how to properly save, upload, and download files is critical. Of course, it is equally important that you know how to get around on the internet.

Your institution should, at the very minimum, provide training on how to use the LMS that they have adopted. Keep in mind, however, that these are only the technical basics of building an online course. The larger challenge is the redesign of your onsite course content for effective online teaching and learning.

Note: We are not recommending any particular LMS. In fact, you can teach an online course without even using an LMS.

Look at the two screenshots below (see Figure 1.1). The first is a sample of a course screen with the LMS menus visible. In this case, they surround a central rectangle containing the course information. The teacher does not usually have any control over the design of the outer area containing the LMS menu.

In the second screenshot, we have shown only that part of the course created by the teacher. This is what we address in this book. Should we need to refer to the use of LMS tools or menus, we will try to generalize rather than mention a specific LMS.

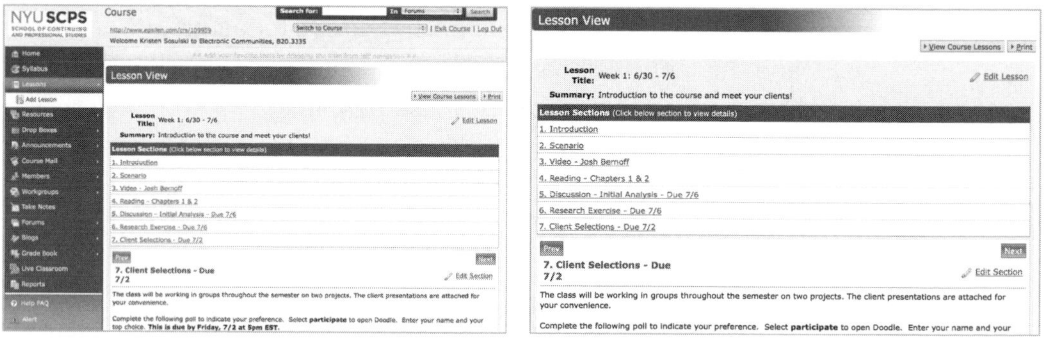

Figure 1.1 *Left*: Course content within an LMS; *Right*: LMS menus screened out
Reprinted with permission

These examples are from Kristen Sosulski's Electronic Communities course at NYU. We have included teacher profiles throughout this book for our featured teachers.

Kristen Sosulski, Clinical Assistant Professor at NYU. Online, Kristen teaches courses in social media, collaboration, virtual community building, and business research methods to undergraduate and graduate students.

Kristen's course content is from two online courses designed and taught by her: **Collaboration Technologies** and **Electronic Communities**. In her courses, Kristen assigns online articles, case studies, and books by current authors in the field. To complement this, her online learners work on several collaborative projects throughout the semester, interact with class guests, and write a critique of the current commentary around social media. Students lead interactive presentations and shape the direction of the course with their interests in business, digital media, and communications.

Figure 1.2

Note: Throughout this guide we use screenshots from various LMSs. We also designed our own screenshots to simply highlight some of the common LMS features and display formats. Both the authentic and handmade screenshots are examples of the standards we espouse throughout the guide.

Visit the book website, where you can view a movie of teachers walking you through an LMS. This should help you become familiar with LMS menus and navigation.

1.4 Features of a Learning Management System

Tip
The organization of the website mirrors that of the book.

Tables 1.1 and 1.2 list the asynchronous and synchronous features of an LMS that you might choose to use in teaching your online course. Refer to Chapter 2 for a walk through of the basic asynchronous features of an online course. The example we use is from a Macroeconomics course with another one of our featured online teachers, Joelle Scally. Throughout this book we incorporate examples from quantitative, humanities, skills-based, and professional fields.

Table 1.1 Sample Learning Management System features list—asynchronous

Feature	Definition
Syllabus	An overview of the course in outline form. It includes objectives, requirements, etc.
Calendar	Schedule of deadlines and course events
Teacher Announcements	Teacher updates and reminders. In an online course they usually appear upon entering the LMS
Course Email	Correspondence between course members
Lessons	Content sections usually organized by topic
Discussion Forums	Ongoing online voice or text discussions
Wiki	An online environment that can be shared and edited by all members of a collaborative team
Blog	An online space where one author creates a posting (e.g. article, critique, some type of narrative) and others comment
Testing/Quizzing	Assessments that determine how successfully outcomes have been achieved. Ungraded self-assessments help learners adjust the pace of and reflect on their learning

Table 1.2 Sample Learning Management System features list—synchronous

Tool	Definition
Chat	An online exchange of text comments and remarks between two or more participants in real time
Live Classroom/ Live Meeting	Online class sessions in which the teacher and all members are there at the same time and communicate using voice and video

1.5   Time—Onsite vs. Online

One of the first challenges for teachers new to the online environment is to understand how time works when teaching online.

When teaching onsite in a classroom, we think in terms of very specific and clearly defined periods of time needed for: planning, preparation, class sessions, getting to and from class, feedback on assignments, and office hours.

For example, U.S. universities generally define classes in terms of credits. Each credit represents 15 hours of class time. Most courses are 3 credits, or 45 classroom hours, long. Whether the class is 6 or 8 or 15 weeks long, a standard 3-credit class will usually have 45 hours of classroom time. In addition, it is expected that a learner will do an additional 2 to 3 hours of outside work per classroom hour. So, for a learner:

3-credit class = 45 classroom hours + approximately 90 hours outside of class

3-credit class = approximately 135 hours in total

The hours per week vary depending upon the length (in weeks) of the course.

But what happens to this time frame when you teach a 3-credit asynchronous online class? Nothing is scheduled.

As with an onsite course, a 3-credit online course can be taught within a variety of time frames: 15 weeks, 9 weeks, 5 weeks, etc. (see Table 1.3). As with an onsite course, a

Table 1.3 Learning hours per week by length of class in weeks

Weeks	Hours in class per week	Hours outside of class per week	Total hours
15	3	6	135
9	5	10	135
5	9	18	135

3-credit online course offered over 5 weeks will require more time per week than a 15-week course.

What Is a Week Online?

An online course's time frame is defined in terms of weeks, as it is in an onsite course. The teacher plans for how much time learners should be spending on work and participation. It should be equal to the time spent for its onsite equivalent. However, the actual time the learner spends sitting at a computer does not correlate to the amount of time spent sitting in a classroom.

The **actual** time the learner spends online in an asynchronous online class is not taken into consideration. Why not? Well, for example, one learner may spend an hour writing out responses or preparing a slide presentation offline, then cut and paste it in when online. The 2–3 minutes the student spends online putting up the material does not represent the amount of time they have spent working on the presentation. They may also write their discussion forum responses offline, then cut and paste them in.

Another student may do a great deal of their writing while they are online in the course environment. Learners will vary in how much time they actually spend online. **While class participation is important, class session time is no longer a factor.**

Online "attendance" is determined by looking at both the quantity and quality of learner participation. Requirements for participation are stated very clearly in the syllabus (see Chapter 9).

Flexibility and Convenience

When teachers begin thinking about transforming their class to online they often feel uncertain about how to plan for time. One thing for certain, unless a class is in real time (synchronous) or blended, with part of it occurring at a set time either onsite or online in real time, "class time" is flexible for both the teacher and the learner.

Tip

Make learners aware early on that deadlines will help to structure their time in an online course. Continue to remind them of this through online course announcements that are posted in the LMS and simultaneously emailed to students.

Because the course is asynchronous, **you can go online any time day or night, whenever it is convenient for you.** This kind of flexibility appeals to people with other commitments such as work or families.

This flexibility is also helpful if you are working with an international class. Learners and teachers can go online whenever convenient, working within their local time zones across the globe.

There are, of course, **deadlines and guidelines**. These play a crucial structuring role in an otherwise open time frame.

Note: Deadlines in an international class need to be stated in a set time zone (e.g. an assignment may be due on May 15 at noon GMT (Greenwich Mean Time—UK) or EST (eastern standard time—east coast, US). The learners are responsible for calculating what that means in their local time frame.

Tip
Use a website application that converts time zones, such as http://timezone guide.com.

What's the Catch?

The downside of flexibility and convenience is the absence of the kind of structure that you have when planning for classes scheduled at a set time. Here are two key points that will help with this:

- **In the end, the online course must be equal in content and challenge to the onsite course.** Content and learner work should be equal in both courses.

- **The course content is driven by the identical learning outcomes that drive the onsite course.** Use the learning outcomes as a check.

The online process is outcome- and content-driven. A week's content for a 15-week online course is the same as its onsite equivalent.

 Course material is sufficient and directly related to learning outcomes.

 Learning outcomes for an online course are identical to those of the onsite version.

How Much Time Does Online Teaching and Learning Take?

Time spent on online teaching and learning is difficult to estimate. Generally speaking, it takes more time than the onsite equivalent. Of course, an argument can be made that much, or all, of this extra time is regained since you are not traveling back and forth to class.

A teacher goes online regularly. Depending on his schedule, style and working preferences, a teacher may go online once a day, or several times a day for shorter periods, or do something in between. Sometimes he will be just "checking in" to see how things are going. Other times he will spend an hour or more on online activities: posting announcements, initiating discussions, reading, and/or responding to learners. There may be a day when he goes online once, for only 20 minutes, and then, on another day, he may spend 2 to 3 hours online. He might download learner work and check it, make notes, then go online to respond when it's more convenient.

Also, online work can be portable. The teacher might, for example, go through homework checks or read learner posts on a smartphone or on paper while on a bus. Flexibility and portability can also make online teaching feel like less time is spent.

What is the Teacher Doing with Her Time?

The following is most likely how a teacher spends time (assuming she is both designing and teaching the course):

- **Designing the course**. Ideally this is done before the course begins. This part of the process is what we are covering in this guide.

- **Posting new material**. The teacher is putting up announcements, new learning material, introducing a new discussion topic, initiating a new kind of activity, etc., as needed.

- **Checking in on learner interactions, participation, and work**. This most typically happens in a discussion forum where learners are responding to new material, the teacher's posts and other learners' posts. It is also possible that this is happening in other ways and "places" online such as in wikis, the teacher's blog, learners' blogs, group "spaces," presentation areas, etc.

- **Giving feedback on assignments**. Learner assignments require feedback. The time spent on this should be about the same as it is in an onsite course.

- **Class management**. Activities such as setting up places for learners to submit their work and communicate (discussion forum threads, drop box folders, chat rooms, etc.), sending out reminders of assignments that are due, grouping/pairing learners for team projects, and introducing new assignments and requirements.

Saving Time

One of the most important factors in saving time comes up during the course-building stage. While the course design and implementation of standards may require more upfront time, it can save time in the end. The very first time you create an online course may be quite time consuming. Each time that course is taught again, you will only be revising and updating. This will get easier as you gain experience.

Our goal in this book is to save you as much time as possible during the course-building stage. We do this by emphasizing:

- planning

- organization

- consistency

- simplicity and clarity of language and instructions

- easy access to or basic production of images, audio, and video

- models of a variety of activities and assessments, and

- the use of organizing templates.

 You will see this icon whenever we cover a topic that helps you save time during the course-development process.

1.6 Summary and Standards

In this chapter we provided an orientation for online teaching and learning. The differences between onsite and online teaching were outlined, as well as the key characteristics of teaching online.

☐ Course material is sufficient and directly related to learning outcomes.

☐ Learning outcomes for an online course are identical to those of the onsite version.

Chapter 2

Elements of an Online Course: A Tour

This chapter covers the basic features available within most learning management systems (LMSs). The names of the tools/features may vary across LMSs. We try to cover the most common alternatives.

While it is certainly possible to teach an online course without an LMS, their use is so widespread that we felt it was necessary to provide a general overview of LMS features.

The illustrations in this chapter are taken from an online course in Macroeconomics at NYU. The course "introduces the methods and disciplines of economics through an examination of the American system. Topics include: national income analysis, business fluctuations, fiscal policies, principles of money and banking, the economics of the corporation, and resource allocation" (New York University School of Continuing and Professional Studies, 2010). Epsilen was the LMS used.

Note: We did not modify the screenshots for print readability in this chapter. We did this to give you a sense of the authentic look of an LMS.

Table 2.1 (see page 41) presents the elements you normally need to build your online course. It lists all of the features of the LMS that need to be set up before the course goes live. We've also referenced the chapters that are most appropriate for you to review for each item.

2.1 Meet the Teacher

We'll begin by introducing you to the teacher who designed the content we are using in this section.

Joelle Scally, Adjunct Instructor, NYU, School of Continuing and Professional Studies. Joelle teaches an undergraduate online course in **Macroeconomics** to adult learners. She works as an economic analyst at the Federal Reserve Bank of New York.

In her course, Joelle uses many forms of online assessment, including midterm and final exams, problem sets, and collaborative projects and activities using wikis and blogs. In addition, Joelle holds weekly discussions with her students via the **forum** around current issues in macroeconomics such as fiscal policy.

Personal Perspective
Joelle Scally

Kristen: Joelle, can you describe any challenges you encountered teaching a quantitative subject online and how you overcame them?

Joelle: Teaching a quantitative subject online poses its own set of challenges. First, students join the course with a wide range of math ability. This challenge can be even more striking in adult learners, since, in some cases, many years have passed since a student's last math class. Without the ability to monitor students' facial expressions and questions in real time, it isn't always easy to know if the class work is within the students' ability level. Providing examples, sample questions, and very specific, step-by-step guidance to complicated quantitative questions on both problem sets and sample exams for students is very helpful, and creates a more instructive experience for students.

Another challenge in teaching quantitative courses online is that students submit assignments electronically. If graphing or any complicated notation is necessary, completing the problem can become extremely onerous without a scanner. While access to a scanner was required, minimizing these types of problems and instead assigning problems where students were asked to evaluate and analyze provided graphs was helpful.

We selected Joelle Scally's course as an example for this book because she used various features of the LMS to teach and design her online course. Also, we wanted readers to see examples of how a quantitative course can be designed for online.

2.2 A Course Tour

There are many features available in LMSs to allow you to create a rich and dynamic course. These features are only as good as the content and pedagogical approaches that are employed (see Figure 2.1).

Some of the **basic features in an LMS** toolbar are:

- announcements
- syllabus
- lessons
- discussion forums
- drop boxes/assignment upload
- resources
- grade book
- course email, and
- resources.

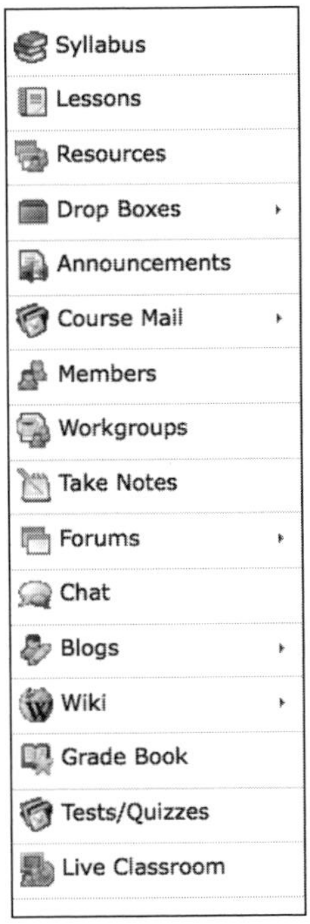

These features should be standard to any LMS and teachers should plan to use them in their online courses.

Many LMSs are equipped with **more advanced features** that facilitate student-centered learning and communication. These may include:

- blogs
- wikis
- tests and quizzes
- workgroups, and
- portfolios.

Figure 2.1
LMS course toolbar

We'll introduce you to the basic features and some of the advanced features to orient you to your new teaching space! Let's review these features and explore how they are used.

Announcements

Teacher announcements are usually the first thing students see when entering an online course within an LMS.

Welcome to the course!

My name is Joelle Scally—I will be the instructor for this course. If you'd like to read more about me, my bio can be found at: www.epsilen.com/jwm2106.

This is an asynchronous online course, which means we won't often have an official meeting time or place (actual or virtual). Instead, the success of this course depends on you keeping up with the syllabus, your level of involvement with this site and the online activities that I've planned.

Even though it is asynchronous, it does not mean that there is no time component—in fact, the success of many of the activities depends on your participation in a timely manner.

Let's get to know one another. If you have not already done so, please post a message in the "Introduce Yourself" forum, describing your background, expectations for this course, and any concerns you may have about online learning or macroeconomics.

I am looking forward to the course. Macroeconomics is a passion of mine, and I hope it will be a passion of yours as well!

Best regards,

Joelle

Figure 2.2
An online welcome announcement

The announcements feature is the place where the teacher communicates important updates to the class. When the teacher posts an announcement, it will be waiting for students to read it whenever they enter the online course environment. See Figure 2.2 for Joelle's "welcome announcement" to students.

Syllabus

After reading the course announcements, the students review the course syllabus.

The **syllabus** feature is an essential component of the course environment. It **provides structure for the course and outlines course expectations**. When students enter your course for the first time, they should review the syllabus to familiarize themselves with the course requirements. See Figure 2.3 for an example.

Instructor Joelle Scally
Email jwm2106@nyu.edu
Course Number Y10.0301, Semester Fall 2010, Office Hours Email is preferred, and I will answer emails within 24 hours.

Course Description

This course will introduce the discipline of economics through a study of the American and global system. Topics will include national accounting, employment, unemployment, interest rates, and inflation. We will also discuss economic policy (monetary and fiscal), international trade and exchange rates, and some of the major macroeconomic models.

Additionally, given the current financial crisis and "uncharted waters" that the economy is currently in, it is absolutely critical that students finish the course with some understanding of this crisis.

Communication Strategy

Because asynchronous online courses are so disconnected, there are other requirements for this course to connect us more closely:

1) You must have a clear photo set for your Epsilen profile photo!
2) I expect you to be responsive to my emails -- if I email you, please write me back within 48 hours. Because of the nature of the course, if you do not respond to my respond to my emails, this is like being absent from class.

Course Objectives

At the end of this course, all students should understand:

- the difference between micro and macroeconomics
- the concept of supply and demand
- fiscal and monetary policy
- the role of money and the Federal Reserve system
- important economic data (National Income and Product Accounts, price index, etc) and be able to read and understand news reports on this data

Required Readings

Required Textbook:

Brief Principles of Macroeconomics, 5th Ed.
by N. Gregory Mankiw

Figure 2.3 An online course syllabus (only a partial syllabus is shown)

Reprinted with permission

Lessons

Students review the week-by-week (or unit-by-unit) course lessons.

Online lessons replace the **lectures**, **discussions**, and **activities** that may take place in an onsite classroom.

The lessons are the core instructional containers for your course. You may post a lesson for each unit of instruction. The lessons should lead the students through the course's learning outcomes. See Figure 2.4 for a partial listing of lessons. The students click on the lesson title (i.e. "WEEK 01: 09/08 to 09/14—Introducing Economics") to see (in this case) the lesson outcome and summary (see Figure 2.5).

Course Lessons

Select a lesson from the list below.

Title	Start Date
WEEK 01: 09/07 to 09/13 - Introducing Economics Chapters 1 & 2	08/29/2010
WEEK 02: 09/14 to 09/20 - Trade, Consumption, & Production Chapter 3	09/14/2010
WEEK 03: 09/21 to 09/26 - Supply & Demand Chapter 4	09/21/2010
WEEK 04: 09/28 to 10/04 - Measurements: National Income Chapter 5	09/28/2010
WEEK 05: 10/05 to 10/11 - Measurements: The Cost of Living Chapter 6	10/05/2010
WEEK 06: 10/12 to 10/18 - Productivity & Growth Chapter 7	10/12/2010

Figure 2.4 A (partial) listing of the lessons for each week of the online course

Reprinted with permission

Each lesson is broken down into sections. Figure 2.5 presents the sections of a weekly lesson. Students click on each section to get to the content.

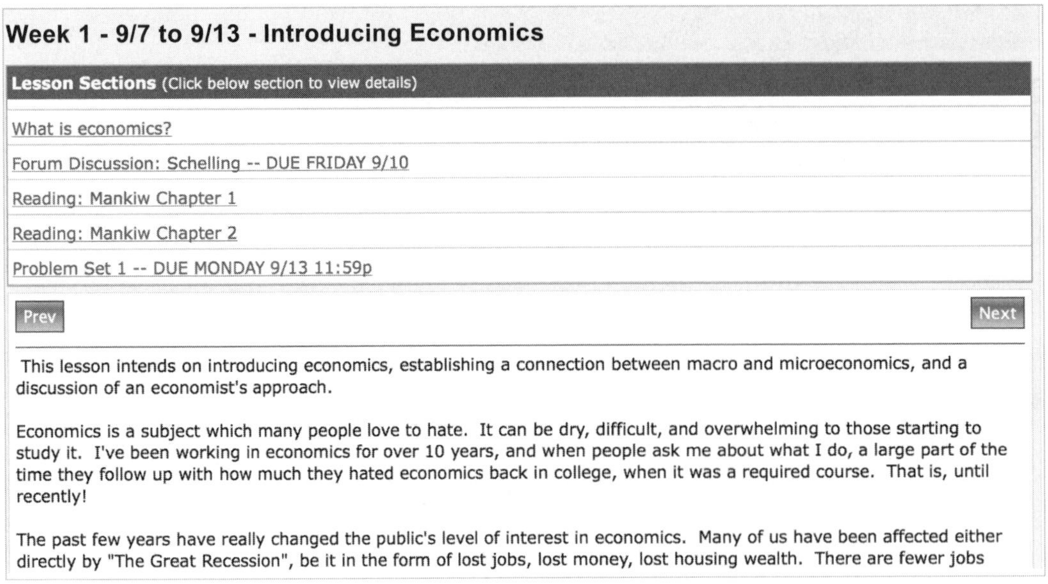

Week 1 - 9/7 to 9/13 - Introducing Economics

Lesson Sections (Click below section to view details)

What is economics?

Forum Discussion: Schelling -- DUE FRIDAY 9/10

Reading: Mankiw Chapter 1

Reading: Mankiw Chapter 2

Problem Set 1 -- DUE MONDAY 9/13 11:59p

Prev   Next

This lesson intends on introducing economics, establishing a connection between macro and microeconomics, and a discussion of an economist's approach.

Economics is a subject which many people love to hate. It can be dry, difficult, and overwhelming to those starting to study it. I've been working in economics for over 10 years, and when people ask me about what I do, a large part of the time they follow up with how much they hated economics back in college, when it was a required course. That is, until recently!

The past few years have really changed the public's level of interest in economics. Many of us have been affected either directly by "The Great Recession", be it in the form of lost jobs, lost money, lost housing wealth. There are fewer jobs

Figure 2.5 The course content sections for a weekly lesson

Reprinted with permission

Discussion Forums

Students go to the discussion forums to participate in the online class discussion. They are directed to the forum from the lesson (see Figure 2.5).

The forums feature is an asynchronous communication tool that allows for the exchange of ideas through the use of a message board format. The structure of most discussion forums is based on a participant's ability to post messages or reply to messages posted by other participants.

Communication between participants is initiated when someone, usually the moderator, posts a topic or question for discussion. Based upon this first post, participants begin to communicate with one another by responding to the original post or to the posts of other participants. Discussion forums are used to promote conversations between students and the teacher. Figure 2.6 is an example of a discussion forum topic posted by Joelle for the students to discuss.

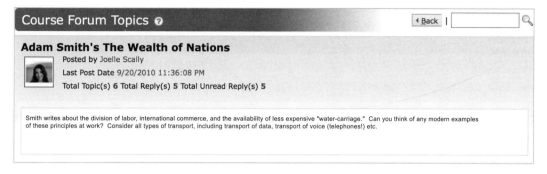

Figure 2.6 An online class discussion topic posted by the teacher in the discussion forum
Reprinted with permission

Drop Boxes/Assignment Upload

To submit assignments, the teacher may require the students to upload their documents to an online drop box or the assignments section of the LMS.

A drop box is a digital space in which documents, presentations, links to websites, and more can be uploaded by the students and accessed by the teacher. You may create and use a drop box to have students submit and store assignments and projects for group or instructor review. Figure 2.7 is an example of four drop boxes that Joelle set up for students to upload their problem-set assignments.

Drop Boxes ❷

Drop Box	Description	Files
Problem Set 1 - Due 9/13 11:59p	Please upload problem set 1 here.	13
Problem Set 2 - Due 09/20 11:59p	Please upload problem set 2 here	6
Problem Set 3 - Due 09/27 11:59p	Please upload problem set 3 here.	0
Problem Set 4 - Due 10/04 11:59p	Please upload problem set 4 here.	0

Figure 2.7 Drop boxes set up by the teacher to collect problem-set assignments from students

Assignment	Points	
Problem Set 1 1.44% of Final Grade	78	/ 100.00
Problem Set 2 1.44% of Final Grade	80	/ 100.00
Problem Set 3 1.44% of Final Grade	95	/ 100.00
Problem Set 4 1.44% of Final Grade	88	/ 100.00
Problem Set 5 1.44% of Final Grade	100	/ 100.00

Figure 2.8
The online grade book in an LMS

Reprinted with permission

Grade Book

The teacher uses the online grade book to communicate grades and feedback to learners.

The **grade book** feature is a tool that displays students' attendance, participation, readings, assignments, and project grades. This feature **enables the teacher and the students to review and track academic progress throughout the semester**.

See Figure 2.8 for Joelle's online grade book. Notice how the problem-set assignment titles correspond to those in the drop box in Figure 2.7.

 For more examples of grade books, see the website.

Course Mail

The teacher may use the course mail feature to send out important messages to students. This is similar to course announcements. Mail can be sent to individual students or the entire class. It can be more time-sensitive than announcements since students probably check their email more frequently than they go into their online class.

The course email feature is an asynchronous communication tool that enables the teacher to send messages to class members and also view received, archived, or sent course-related messages. Course email uses the same features as other email systems in that it allows users to send messages to single or multiple users, which are then stored in their mailbox until deleted. See Figure 2.9 for Joelle's course mail, which archives all her sent messages to students regarding the final exam.

Course Mail ❷

Use Course Mail to send a new Message and view your received, archived and sent messages for this course.

| Course Mail | Archived | Sent | | ▸ Send a New Message |

Select: Read | Unread   Delete Selected | Archive Selected | Mark as Read | Mark as Unread   [Sort by... ⬍]

■ From	Subject	Received Date	Action
Joelle Scally Faculty nyu	Welcome to week...	9/14/2010 9:06:15 AM	🔍 👥 ✓ 🖺 🗑
Joelle Scally Faculty nyu	some notes...	9/11/2010 11:24:16 AM	🔍 👥 ✓ 🖺 🗑
Joelle Scally Faculty nyu	Macroeconomics ...	9/7/2010 2:27:38 PM	🔍 👥 ✓ 🖺 🗑

Figure 2.9
The course mail feature of an LMS

Reprinted with permission

Resources

In an online course, digital course readings and references are organized in a section commonly referred to as "resources."

The **"resources" feature stores all types of digital and online materials that students are required to review**, including readings, websites, games, images, sound recordings, and video. To enable easy access to these resources, the teacher may provide links to them within the lessons. In addition, other resources may just appear within the lessons themselves. This is especially true for short video and audio clips, and images.

Joelle uses the resources section to post answers to problem sets, provide practice mid-term and final exam questions, and multimedia resources (see Figure 2.10).

Blogs

The **blogs feature is an online journal that enables the teacher and the students to post commentary on course questions, topics, and projects**. A single writer serves as the administrator of the blog and is usually the only editor of its content.

Resources			
Category	**Title**	**Description**	**File/Url**
Audios / Videos	Explanation of Production Possibilities Frontier	This YouYube video has a very nice, clear explanat... Read more about This YouYube..	http://www.youtube.c...
Publications	Micromotives & Macrobehavior	This is the reading for the first week, in PDF for... Read more about This is..	Schelling ....or CH1...
Presentations	A Word on the Economy: Why Is the Country Facing a Financial Crisis?	Presentation from the Federal Reserve Bank of St. ... Read more about Presentation from..	http://www.stlouisfe...

Figure 2.10

The resources section of an LMS

Reprinted with permission (Spelling error in original.)

Users are able to set up and edit their blogs for the course, and also post comments on other blogs attached to the course. Entries are displayed in reverse chronological order, and include a time and date stamp that enables readers to see when a new comment has been posted.

Blogs offer teachers and students the ability to add commentary to the general course discussion and assignments. Figure 2.11 is an example of a blog posted by Joelle illustrating price increases since 1995.

 See the website for examples of blogs and explanations of how they are used.

Wikis

The **wiki feature is a communal space in which the teacher and the students are able to post and edit content in order to create a collaborative information resource**. A wiki works upon the premise that users will add, edit, and structure content.

A wiki does not require that users employ a fixed structure for edits and format. Instead, through collaboration, users generate guidelines to structure the content, which may change as the wiki is developed. Ensuring that the structure

View Blog Entry   ◄ Back |

⭐ **Price Increases since 1995 [Sample CPI Blog]**

Posted by Joelle Scally
Posted on MON 10/5/2009 11:14:58 PM

Since I graduated from high school in 1995, I thought it would be interesting to find out the prices of items compare now to then. **So, let's imagine (dream) that I received a very luxurious watch as a graduation gift.** This watch currently retails for $6,050. How much did my benefactor pay for this watch? We know that:

```
amount in today's dollars = amount in year T dollars * (price level today / price level in year T)
```

So, to fill in the variables:

```
2009_watch_price = 1995_watch_price * (2009cpi / 1995cpi)
```

But, we don't know the 1995_watch_price, so we have to get that by itself with a little algebra. Just solve for 1995_watch_price:

```
(1995cpi / 2009cpi) * 2009_watch_price = 1995_watch_price
```

Here's a table with the relevant data:

Time	Watch Price	CPI for Watches
June 1995	???	127.000
August 2009	$6,050.00	114.603

Notice that the CPI has actually decreased, implying that the price for watches has actually gone done in the past 14 years! To find out how much my gifter may have paid: (127.000 / 114.603) * 6050 = $6,704.45

Figure 2.11 A teacher-led blog illustrating price increases since 1995

Reprinted with permission

View Course Wiki ❓   ◄ Back |

Gains from Trade   Version - 1

Joelle Scally, Administrator Created On 9/14/2010 9:00:33 AM
Collaborative document about comparative advantage and gains from trade.

Comparative Advantage/Gains from Trade

Definition:

<fill in here>

Who Benefits?:

<fill in here>

Examples of agricultural gains from intrastate trade:

California is blessed with fertile soil and an excellent climate, and consequently produces a huge amount of the nation's produce, including certain items which cannot be grown in other states. According to the Agricultural Statistical Review of the California Agricultural Resource Directory 2008-2009, California is the largest producer of a dizzying number of crops in the US, including Artichokes, Celery, Lemons, Strawberries, among 75 others! When you look at the growing season for these, it's easy to understand how they lead, with in many cases a growing season which lasts year-round. California grows 99% of the artichokes in the United States, so chances are, an artichoke craving in New York is likely to be satisfied by a California artichoke -- artichokes do not grow in New York.

Figure 2.12 An example of a course assignment using a wiki

Reprinted with permission

of the wiki does not become too unwieldy depends upon the goals of the wiki assignment. See Figure 2.12 for an example of an activity Joelle devised using the course wiki.

 See the website for examples of wikis and explanations of how they are used.

Tests and Quizzes

Many LMSs are equipped with assessment tools for creating online tests. Typically these tests provide computer-generated feedback to the learners. Figure 2.13 is a partial midterm example in Joelle's course. Notice how you can include various question types and formats. See Chapter 5 for additional examples.

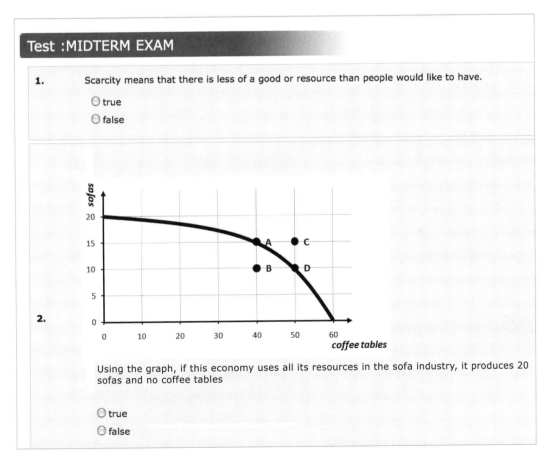

Figure 2.13 An online midterm exam

Workgroups

The **workgroups feature is a space in which the teacher can assign the students to different groups for course discussions, development and presentation of assignments, and projects**. This is a shared class space in which students are able to post updates and information to other group members, upload and store project files, and create interactive and collaborative projects. See Figure 2.14 for the features of an online workgroup.

Note: Joelle did not use workgroups in her online course.

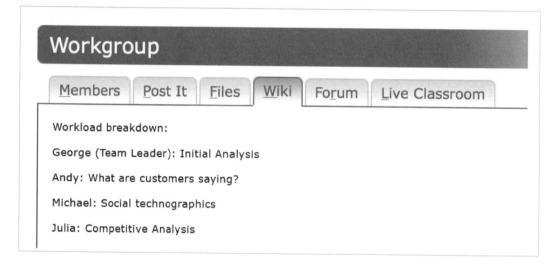

Figure 2.14 The features of an online workgroup from another online class
Reprinted with permission

 ## Summary

The features introduced in this chapter are only a sampling of the tools found within many LMSs. While you are becoming acquainted with your institution's system, you should also review the documentation available. Refer to Table 2.1 for an easy-to-use checklist of the main features of the LMS that the teacher can use to create and set up an online course.

Table 2.1 LMS features that are commonly used for an online course

LMS Feature	Item	Description	Chapters
Announce-ments	Welcome announcement	Create an announcement that welcomes students to the course in a conversational tone, briefly describes the course, directs students to read the syllabus, describes the course format, and how the course is organized in the LMS, and directs students to the "Introduce Yourself" forum.	2, 10, App. B
Forums	Discussions	Set up the discussion forum threads for your online discussions. These should be organized by lesson.	2, 5, 7, App. B
Syllabus	Syllabus components (see Table 9.1)	• Basic course information • Communication strategy • Course time frame and format • Assignments • Activity grade percentages • Criteria for class participation • Technical requirements and support • Course outline	1, 3, 5, 7, 9, App. B
Various Lessons	1 or more lessons created for each unit of the course	A lesson should be created for each week of the course. The lesson should at least include the following: • Lesson title with start and end dates • Introduction with learning outcomes • Required and recommended readings • Assignments with due dates and times • Summary	5, 6, 8, 9, 10, App. B
Resources	Linked online material and uploaded files	The online readings and relevant materials are linked and/or uploaded to the resources section of the site. Link the relevant resources to each module.	6, 8, 10
Drop Boxes/ Assignment Submission Area	Drop box for submission of student assignments	For assignments that require students to submit papers or projects, create a drop box for each assignment.	7, 10
Blogs, Wikis, and Workgroups	Collaboration tools	For activities that rely on the use of collaborative tools, such as blogs, wikis, and workgroups, set up those spaces in the LMS.	3, 5, 7, 10

Chapter 3   Language and Writing Style

Power—Use less, gain more.

Maeda (2006), 3rd law of simplicity

Clear, concise writing addresses the needs of all types of online learners. It removes one more barrier to good communication and understanding. This chapter reviews the basic pitfalls to avoid and techniques to embrace when writing for your online class. The chapter also includes a section on writing instructions for activities and course announcements.

3.1   Rationales for Clear, Concise Writing

Clear, concise writing always supports good communication and learning.

Using clear, concise writing models an accessible style that learners might emulate. Whatever the subject, teachers may also find that commenting on learners' writing advances the learning process. The tone used in such exchanges should be supportive.

3.2   Writing Style

> Less is more.
>
> Motto of Ludwig Mies van der Rohe

The following advice on writing style has been around for a while but is still relevant today:

> A sentence should contain no unnecessary words, a paragraph no unnecessary sentences... This requires not that the writer make all his sentences short, or that he avoid all detail and treat his subject only in outline, but that every word tell.
>
> Strunk, Jr. (1918)

In other words, keep it simple! This is not always as easy as it sounds. Sometimes the only way to get there is to take some time to edit carefully until it just becomes natural to write clearly and concisely.

 The writing style is clear, concise, and direct.

3.3 Paragraphs

Enormous blocks of print look formidable to a reader. He has a certain reluctance to tackle them; he can lose his way in them. Therefore breaking a paragraph in two, even though it is not necessary to do so for sense, meaning, or logical development, is often a visual help.

Strunk, Jr. (1918)

This is especially true online. We will revisit the topic of short paragraphs again when we get to Chapter 8.

3.4 Sentences

Sentences should be concise and clear. Let's look at some examples for simplifying, inspired by Strunk and White:

Tom is the type of person who **likes to eat out with a group** of friends.
Tom likes to eat out with friends.

The reason why **I don't go out alone at night is that I'm afraid to do so**.
I'm afraid to go out alone at night.

And here are some examples from rewrites from this guide:

Once the class begins the teacher's role is to **focus on learner participation and assessment**.
Once the class begins the teacher focuses on learner participation and assessment.

There are **some learners** that may **fall into more than one** of these **categories**.
Some learners fall into more than one category.

 Sentences and paragraphs are brief and to the point.

3.5 Words and Phrases

Below is the classic set of instructions on the use of words in writing:

> [O]ne can often be in doubt about the effect of a word or a phrase, and one needs rules that one can rely on when instinct fails. I think the following rules will cover most cases:
>
> i. Never use a metaphor, simile or other figure of speech which you are used to seeing in print.
> ii. Never use a long word where a short one will do.
> iii. If it is possible to cut a word out, always cut it out.
> iv. Never use the passive where you can use the active.
> v. Never use a foreign phrase, a scientific word or a jargon word if you can think of an everyday English equivalent...
>
> Orwell (1946)

Avoid Jargon

Jargon, unlike technical terms, can be replaced by standard English words and phrases. Obviously, avoiding jargon makes your content understandable to more people.

Using jargon may mean that a learner who is not familiar with the term will either guess at the meaning, just ignore it, or stop what they are doing to look it up. The former two options may lead to misunderstanding. The latter option breaks the flow of concentration on the topic.

Avoid Colloquialisms

While it is possible that your students will be from the same dialect group, all speaking the same first language, it is unlikely. Your language and tone can be informal without being casual. Again, by avoiding colloquialisms you widen the circle of learners who will understand. The class will also feel more inclusive.

Avoid Clichés and Tired Phrases

Well-worn phrases or clichés lose their meaning with so much use. Try making the point in your own words or by using your own devices. Another excellent reason to avoid tired phrases is that they may seem alien and even nonsensical in other parts of the world where people have learned another dialect or form of English. Even native English speakers, living in the country where these phrases originated, may be confused by clichés or well-worn similes or metaphors.

☑ Familiar or common words are used when possible.

☑ Jargon, clichés, and colloquial and idiomatic expressions are avoided.

Explain Acronyms

Acronyms are tricky. It's simply not efficient to write out the full names of every organization, field, etc. Give the full name along with the acronym the first time it is mentioned. However, you cannot assume that the learner will recognize the acronym the next time she sees it. The full name should always be within reach either in an easily accessible glossary or somewhere close by within the learning segment.

> e.g. LMS = learning management system

> e.g. APA = American Psychological Association

Provide a Glossary or Definitions if Needed

However much you succeed at simplifying your language, learners may still need a glossary. Access to the definition of a word, term, or acronym should be immediate.

The most immediate access possible is to click on the word and see the definition appear. This could happen, for example, by creating a hyperlink to its definition. If this is not possible, the definition might just be included somewhere on the same page, perhaps in a text box.

A glossary that requires the learner to leave what they are reading to get to a definition that is two or more clicks away is pedagogically unsound. Refer to Chapter 5 for an example of an activity where students build a shared class glossary using a wiki.

If the above suggestions are not possible, consider giving the students the special terms in the introduction of the lesson, as Scott Thornbury does (see page 157). This allows the students to look them up before they begin the lesson.

 The meaning of special terms, abbreviations, and acronyms is easy to access.

3.6 Tone

> When developing presentations ensure that your tone is conversational. People learn better when the words of a multimedia presentation are in conversational style rather than formal style.
>
> Mayer (2005: 6)

Ideally, learners feel comfortable and motivated when they are in the online environment. Using an informal or conversational tone and encouraging students to do the same helps to create a safe environment online.

Difficult discussions, whether teacher-to-learner or learner-to-learner, should be saved for email correspondence. Openly encourage learners to keep conflicts or personal disagreements out of the classroom space.

An announcement on online etiquette, including guidelines on tone and attitude, are best given to learners before the class begins in an orientation or at the beginning of class. This should include suggestions on:

- tone (see above)
- using clear, correct language
- avoiding *flaming* (angry/screaming/using all caps)
- avoiding *sarcasm*, and
- being tolerant.

 A supportive second-person conversational tone is used throughout the course.

3.7 Writing Instructions and Announcements

> The areas where clarity is most crucial are labeling and instructions—the elements that guide users through the functions of a page. Navigation is not a place for unclear language—link labels must be self-explanatory to guide users to their destination. Clarity in form labels is important, too. Ambiguous form labels lead to incorrect data. In general, all instructions should use clear and concise language
>
> Horton (2005)

In an online course, the primary method for communicating with learners about expectations is through writing. Many of things you will be writing are assignment and activity instructions and course announcements.

The **instructions for activities and assignments must be clear and simply stated**. If items are sequenced, use numbers. If they are a list of options, use bullet points. Anticipate the questions that students may ask, and try to include them in the activity and assignment instructions. Instructions for assignments should generally include: due date and time, submission location in the LMS, and grading criteria. Refer to Figure 3.1 for an example (see next page).

3.8 Labeling

It is critically important that labeling on graphs, charts, diagrams, and images is in a typeface that is large enough to read and clearly visible. The label itself should stand out from the background enough to be seen.

☑ Labeling in all presentation materials is accurate, readable, and clear.

Labeling throughout the course should be clearly written, accurate, and readable. If an image or chart is labeled, the words should be placed so that they stand out and are clear. Links should be descriptive so that students understand what they link to.

Final Paper Instructions

Write a 5-page book review of Clay Shirky's *Here Comes Everybody*.

In your review address the following questions:

- Why are tools not enough to foster collaboration?
- A group's complexity grows faster than its size. Explain.
- Define user-generated content.
- Describe and provide examples of the three types of social loss described by Shirky.
- Why are tools such as MeetUp successful?
- Discuss the importance that Shirky places on failure.

Requirements

Upload your paper to the "Final Paper" drop box by 8/5/2010 by 5:00 p.m. EST. The paper must be submitted as a Microsoft Word (.doc) file. Please name your file lastname_firstname.doc.

The paper must be written in 12 point Arial or Times New Roman font. Double-spaced with one inch margins. A title page is required and **does not** count toward total page count. APA style must be followed and all quoted or referenced material from the book must be cited appropriately.

Figure 3.1 An example of instructions for a Final Paper assignment

Course announcements serve as **organizers** for students to understand what they need to do for a given week (see Figure 3.2). Be clear and point students to the areas in the LMS where they can find the information they need. Avoid using course announcements as a way to deliver or introduce new material; the modules/lessons area of the LMS is designed to present the week-by-week details and content. **Announcements should be sent out to the class weekly**.

 Instructions and requirements are stated simply, clearly, and logically.

Dear Class,

Welcome to week 5 of Collaboration Technologies. For this week please continue reading *Here Comes Everybody*. The details are explained in the week 5 lesson.

Later this week I will be posting the final paper assignment. I will make an announcement in the course and send an email notification indicating where you can find the assignment description details.

Please feel free to contact me with any questions! Happy reading!

Best,

Professor Sosulski

Figure 3.2 An example of a course announcement

3.9 Accuracy

It's good practice to give everything you've written a double check for accuracy. It should be relatively error free.

 The course material has been edited for language and grammar.

3.10 Summary and Standards

Keep it simple, clear, and concise.

Style

☐ The writing style is clear, concise, and direct.

☐ Sentences and paragraphs are brief and to the point.

Language

☐ Familiar or common words are used when possible.

☐ Jargon, clichés, and colloquial and idiomatic expressions are avoided.

☐ The meaning of special terms, abbreviations, and acronyms is easy to access.

☐ Labeling in all presentation materials is accurate, readable, and clear.

☐ Instructions and requirements are stated simply, clearly, and logically.

Tone

☐ A supportive second-person conversational tone is used throughout the course.

☐ The course material has been edited for language and grammar.

Chapter 4   Visual Design Basics

Online material should be attractive. This is different than simply clear text and well organized material. It should be graphically appealing. Researchers at the University of British Columbia rated 127 online courses according to 43 criteria. They found that how a course looks can be just as important as the lessons themselves.

Madden (1999)

4.1   Rationales for Good Visual Design

Good design is a lot like clear thinking made visual.

Motto of Edward Tufte

Good visual design supports understanding through simplicity, clarity, and organization. Nothing in the design of the page distracts from communication. **An open, clear, attractive page design enhances communication.**

We learn from Howard Gardner (1993) (see page 71) that we do not all process visual information in the same way. Simply because a medium is visual does not mean that it will automatically appeal to the visual learner. In fact, the visual learner will be very sensitive to dense, confusing visual design.

Personal Perspective

Marjorie Vai

I, as a strongly visual learner, have been completely shut down at times when facing dense text. It's as if I'm looking at a block of some kind of intricate design. When, for some reason, I am obliged to stick to my reading, I can do it but become frustrated by the lack of attention to readability.

You should be aware of this when creating online content. For the visual learner, great blocks of unbroken text online are the equivalent of listening to an onsite teacher reading from a book in a drone—without intonation, stress, rhythm, pauses, illustrations, or nonverbal language.

The same is true when colors are overused. I need to extract understanding and meaning through a great deal of visual noise. This would be like listening to a lecture in a room with a very noisy factory next door. While all educators would agree with this listening example, some are unaware of the effects of the text examples mentioned above on the visual learner.

A highly respected colleague once insisted that a good teacher is a good teacher, whether onsite or online. Well, this is not exactly true. A teacher who is very good in the classroom needs to transform her skills to a different form of delivery. If she is clear and articulate onsite, she transfers that skill by paying attention to her writing, text readability, and using an open layout online. If she is well organized in her presentation, she will want to pay attention to visual layout and organizing cues, such as numbering, bullets, headings, and subheadings, when presenting online. There is a difference. It is an easy adjustment once you are aware of it.

4.2 Visual Design Online

Classroom teachers in some fields depend on using visuals in the classroom (e.g. art, sciences, etc.). When working online, we must keep in mind that content presented in text is visual as well. This text is different than the text in a book because, online, text replaces speaking through a medium that is perceived of as being visual.

Let's also keep in mind that our "digital pros" (see page 15) are used to visual variety. We live in an age when content is reduced, broken up, illustrated. Things move fast. We can discuss the pros and cons of this, but we can't disagree that it has changed the way many think, especially the young.

As with language, the laws that govern good graphic design have been around for a long time. However, they need to be adjusted for the online medium.

There are ways to add stress, rhythm, emphasis, pauses, and room to think in the presentation of online text and page layout. In this chapter we cover text, layout, and graphic elements that enhance the learning experience.

Personal Perspective
Kristen Sosulski

My suggestion: **read this chapter, then read it again**.

In my work, I've noticed that one of the most common oversights of online teachers is their lack of attention to visual and aesthetic design. There are a lot of textual materials in an online course. It's easy to overlook the format of those materials.

The ways that learners interact with the online course is directly related to how well it is organized and designed. **Dense text and unrelated images can overload and overwhelm the learner.** This can impede learning.

4.3 Page Layout

Once you know how to design and manipulate the space outside, inside, and around your content, you'll be able to give your readers a head start... and perhaps even begin to see your own content in a new light.

Boulton (2007)

Above all else, an online layout must be open. Open means that there is enough white space on the page to keep the mind clear, enough white space to allow the online student to feel that they are not overburdened by the task at hand.

☑ **Page layout is uncluttered and open, and includes a significant amount of white space.**

Spaces Surrounding Text

> The opportunity lost by increasing the amount of blank space is gained back with enhanced attention on what remains... When there is less we appreciate everything much more.
>
> Maeda (2006)

The space between lines and paragraphs provides white space. It gives the reader a visual break. The space between paragraphs should be noticeably deeper than the space between lines.

Again, when text is tight and unbroken, the first thing a person sees is a dark gray shape. He must then try to move past that to seek out the words and begin reading. As we noted on page 43, short paragraphs improve readability.

There should also be space to the left and right of the text. This is important when using text boxes.

When text abuts the sides of a text box, it is difficult to read.
Space should be added surrounding the text.

When text abuts the sides of a text box, it is difficult to read.
Space should be added surrounding the text.

☑ **There is sufficient space between lines, paragraphs, and to the right and left of text so that it stands out and is easy to read.**

Line Length

Research shows that reading slows as line lengths begin to exceed the ideal width, because the reader then needs to use the muscles of the eye or neck to track from the end of one line to the beginning of the next line. If the eye must traverse great distances on a page, the reader must hunt for the beginning of the next line.

Lynch & Horton (2009)

Because the size of browser screens can be varied at will, line length can vary. **When lines of text are too long it is difficult to read.** Generally speaking, the ability to vary line lengths is considered a benefit. However, in an environment where learning is an outcome of good readability, you may want to restrict line length.

Restricting the length of lines may not be within your control. You may be working within an LMS that has already predetermined the line length of your content. At times, the best you can do is to recommend that the students keep their browser window as narrow as possible.

Justification

When text is justified on both sides, it can look neater than text that is only justified on the left. However, it is not as readable as left-justified text for two reasons: the spaces between words vary, and/or words are broken at the end of lines with hyphens. Without specifically adjusting the text, line by line, some strange things can happen. You may, at times, notice "rivers" of space flowing down between words. This is distracting. **Always use left-justified text with ragged right margins as we have in this guide.**

☑ Text is left-justified and right margins are ragged.

Headings and Subheadings

On the web, more than any other prose medium, the look of text layout strongly affects how readers relate to written content. The contrast produced by headlines, subheads, lists, and illustrations give users visual "entry points," drawing their eyes down the page and into the content.

Lynch & Horton (2009)

UNITS, Lessons, Sections, Segments,...

Headings and subheadings signal the organization of the content. Each of the examples above has a specific size, typeface, and/or thickness assigned to it. Headings are generally left-justified like the text. **Headings and subheadings organize the content and should be used consistently.**

☑ Headings and subheadings are used consistently to logically organize content.

4.4 Text

When information is presented in its most basic form, it's easy to draw attention to aspects that are important. For example, in a block of text, emphasizing a word or phrase is a matter of changing one attribute: color, typeface, or style. In a simple layout, drawing the eye to an important section can be accomplished by changing one attribute: background color, leading, or typeface. If, however, the page already contains elements of emphasis, highlighting what is important becomes difficult since so many elements are already competing for attention. And if more and more emphasis is added in an effort to make each element stand out, the resulting design is chaotic and confusing.

Horton (2006)

Typefaces

Figure 4.1 is a list of **web-safe typefaces**. That is, these are typefaces that one can count on being accessible on almost all computers. Most likely, these are the typefaces that you will be restricted to using in an LMS.

It is important to keep in mind that typefaces online have a much lower resolution (measured in dots per inch) than typefaces on paper. Therefore, the general rule is to keep it simple, as always!

The first two typefaces listed in Figure 4.1, Georgia and Times New Roman, are **serif** typefaces. This means that there is more detail in the form of serifs. Serifs are small, tail-like extensions that you find on some of the letters. Also, the thickness of the lines may vary in a serif typeface. It has been argued that serif typefaces are more readable on paper because the detail may help to define the letters.

Other typefaces listed in Figure 4.1, such as Arial and Helvetica, are **sans serif** (without serif) typefaces. These are simpler in form. They tend to be more readable online because the resolution is lower. Small details such as serifs may be unclear online.

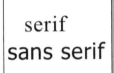

Georgia
Times New Roman
Arial
Helvetica
Tahoma
Trebuchet MS
Verdana
Andale Mono
Courier New
Comic Sans
Impact

serif

sans serif

Figure 4.1
A list of web-safe typefaces

Type Size

Type size is another important factor in online readability. Again, because resolution on a computer screen is much lower than on paper, larger type is easier to read because you have more dots available per inch to define the letters. The letters will be crisper and clearer looking. We recommend that you use at least 12-point type for online. You can see the clear difference between serif and sans serif type at the bottom of Figure 4.1.

 See the resources on the website for more details on type.

 A universal sans serif web typeface (e.g. Verdana) assures access across platforms and enhances screen readability.

 Type size should be large enough to be easily readable by all students.

Bold and Italic—Use Sparingly

Bold type can be used very effectively for emphasis when used sparingly. See examples throughout this guide.

Italic is generally used for titles of works and for instances when words are used in an unusual way. **Italic type is more difficult to read online because of resolution.** Use it sparingly also.

 Bold and italic typefaces are used sparingly only to emphasize important items.

Underlining—Only for Hyperlinks

In an online environment, underlining is used only for hyperlinks.

 Underlining is used only for hyperlinks.

Avoid Using All Caps

All caps should only be used for acronyms. Avoid using them for emphasis. They are not as readable as lower-case letters because they are more uniform in size (e.g. "HIGHLIGHT" vs. "highlight").

 Words in all caps are avoided.

Color—Use with Care

Color can make an impact if it is used with care. Save lighter colors for special emphasis such as highlighting. However, keep in mind that **contrast is an important factor in readability**. Pale yellow works so well for highlighting because it contrasts strongly with black type. If you go darker than that, you begin to sacrifice contrast and, consequently, readability.

The same is true for colored backgrounds. Black against white, or dark blue or black against pale yellow or any other very pale color, will work well. The reverse will work as well (e.g. pale yellow type on a dark blue background). Diminish the contrast and you diminish readability.

Color type is also good for emphasis. A dark color type used for heads can make them pop out.

Keep contrast in mind. Red type may get the learner's attention, but will they be able to read it easily? Keep in mind that learners are looking at a backlit screen in most cases. This is not the same as red print on paper. **Readability depends on contrast.**

There are many ways that color can be used to clarify, enhance, and engage. However, **always keep focused on color's power to distract**. As with all enhancements, it should be used sparingly and with purpose.

Look at Figure 4.2. You can see it on the website in color. The colored names across the top row indicate the background color in each column. The color of the type is indicated in the first column. Looking at it in black and white is very helpful because the contrast, or lack of contrast, is so clear. Keep this chart in mind when using colored type and/or colored backgrounds/highlights.

Notice the use of grays on the pages of this guide. Since we did not have access to color, we used gray the way you might use color. Gray/white/black typefaces, used in combination

background colors							
white	yellow	orange	red	purple	blue	green	black
	white	white	white	white	white	white	white
yellow		yellow	yellow	yellow	yellow	yellow	yellow
orange	orange		orange	orange	orange	orange	orange
red	red	red		red	red	red	red
violet	violet	violet	violet		violet	violet	violet
blue	blue	blue	blue	blue		blue	blue
green	green	green	green	green	green		green
black	black	black	black	black	black	black	

Figure 4.2 A color chart

with certain shapes or graphic elements, signal a certain type of activity, comment, or reading.

 Color is used with purpose.

 There is good contrast between text and background.

4.5 Graphic Elements

Symbols and Icons

Symbols and icons can be very useful in signaling small elements in a website that appear over and over again. For example, here are three of the icons we've used in this book to signal key items that recur:

 To indicate that there is an example or related material on the website.

 To indicate a time-saving suggestion.

☑ or ☐ To signal a standard.

Icons immediately signal the presence of a certain feature. The learner can then scan the material to look for where the particular feature shows up.

Tip
Free icons can be found online. Often, you can just cut and paste them into the text.

You can also use icons to signal certain types of activities. When the student sees the icon they should know what to expect. Icons are helpful for all learners, but especially visual learners.

Another way to signal a certain type of activity is through color-coding. You may use a transparent screen to indicate an assignment or reading, for example. **Look at our featured teacher, Scott Thornbury, whose course example is on the website.** It has a pale gray background color, and an icon and title to indicate a specific kind of activity or reading. This makes the course very easy to follow. As with all graphic elements, they must be used consistently throughout the course.

☑ Visual elements (e.g. icons, shading, and color) are used consistently to distinguish between different types of course elements (e.g. lessons, assignments, audio, and video).

Bullets and Numbers in a Series

Items in a series stand apart when they are bulleted. When the series of items occur in a sequential order, as is the case with most instructions, numbers are used in place of bullets. This distinction is very important.

☑ Use bullets or numbers to set apart items that can be listed.

☑ Numbers are used to identify sequential steps in a task or process. They are also used for rankings and setting priorities.

☑ Bullets are used to highlight a series of items that are not prioritized or sequential.

Example

A judicious use of a selection of visual design elements lets the student instantly know where he is, what he is doing and how things are ordered.

Let's look at an example to illustrate some of the most basic elements. Figure 4.3 (page 62) is a segment of text that needed to be included in the body of an online teacher-training course. The text looks almost like a solid block. The eye tends to see an all-over pattern first. This does not make it very easy to read, especially on a computer screen.

We did the following to rework the text block in Figure 4.4 (page 63):

● **Increased text size**. In this case, we have only increased it by 1 point. It is now 11 points. If this were actually online, 12–14 points would be better.

● Added **space between the letters and lines**.

As Scharle and Szabó (2000) state, *most language teachers have experienced the frustration of investing endless amounts of energy in their students and getting very little response.* Teachers have had students who don't do their homework, are reluctant to speak in the target language or who don't learn from their mistakes. This often happens because students rely on the teacher as the one who should be in charge of whatever happens in the classroom. The answer to this is autonomy. For this to work, we need to have responsible learners. Scharle and Szabó define them as: *those who accept the idea that their own efforts are crucial to progress in learning, and behave accordingly.* They are also willing to cooperate with the teacher and others in the learning group for everyone's benefit.

What makes an autonomous learner?

– Does things beyond what the teacher asks or requests. For instance, may do extra grammar exercises either in print or on line.

– Goes beyond what the teacher presents in class. For example, looks up a new word in a dictionary even if the teacher didn't "teach" it during the lesson.

– Likes to find ways to stay in contact with the target language outside the classroom.

Figure 4.3

A text segment for an online course

Touchstone Online Product Training, Student Centered Learning, Module 1 Academic Background, Student-centered learning including excerpts from Student Centered Classroom, by Leo Jones Copyright © 2010 Cambridge University Press. Reprinted with permission.

- Created **white space between items that can be naturally broken up**. You will most certainly be able to break up, or chunk, text as we have done below. The difference here is that, in addition to breaking material up, we've added more space by isolating some pieces of information, or just adding more space between paragraphs to add more contrast.

- Used **bullets** to emphasize a list of related items. Notice more space is added in front of the bullets.

- Used **bold type for emphasis**. In this case, the use of bold creates a summary of the topic. The basics jump out. As with other elements that are used for emphasis, such as colored text or italics, bold type is only effective if used sparingly. If too much text is in bold, the sense of emphasis is lost.

- Added a **heading**. Colored, bold, or larger type distinguishes the headings from the content, and signals the topic. Headings and subheadings emphasize, distinguish, and organize. It is critical that headings and subheadings are used consistently otherwise they lose their very important organizing function.

Learner Autonomy

As Scharle and Szabó (2000) state, *most language teachers have experienced the frustration of investing endless amounts of energy in their students and getting very little response.*

Teachers have had students who don't do their homework, are reluctant to speak in the target language or who don't learn from their mistakes. This often happens because students rely on the teacher as the one who should be in charge of whatever happens in the classroom.

The answer to this is autonomy.

For this to work, we need to have responsible learners. Scharle and Szabó define them as: those who accept the idea that their own efforts are crucial to progress in learning, and behave accordingly. They are also willing to cooperate with the teacher and others in the learning group for everyone's benefit.

What makes an autonomous learner?

An autonomous learner:

- **Does things beyond what the teacher asks** or requests. For instance, may do extra grammar exercises either in print or on line.

- **Goes beyond what the teacher presents** in class. For example, looks up a new word in a dictionary even if the teacher didn't "teach" it during the lesson.

- Likes to find ways to **stay in contact with the target language outside the classroom**. For example, may regularly keep up with English language sites of interest on the internet.

Figure 4.4 A reworked example of text from Figure 4.3 for an online course

Student Centered Classroom, by Leo Jones Copyright © 2007 Cambridge University Press. Reprinted with permission.

Visual Design Basics in the Online Class

How do you bring these ideas of basic visual design into the online class? The truth is, at times, it may be difficult. You can follow most of the standards we've laid out for type, justification, headings, bullets, and numbers fairly easily. Below is an example of a tool bar for a discussion forum. While LMSs may vary, this one is fairly typical.

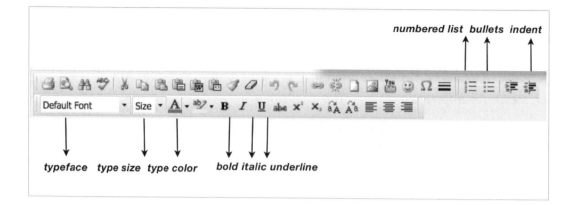

Figure 4.5
A typical editing toolbar in an LMS

We have labeled the buttons that relate to the items in this chapter (see Figure 4.5).

Depending on how rigid your online environment is, the issue of white space and space between lines, letters, and paragraphs may be challenging. In a discussion board text box, the only thing you may be able to do is skip a line before you begin writing, keep your paragraphs short, and skip a line between each paragraph. Be mindful of the impact of visual elements.

4.6 Resources

Tip
If you just begin by making sure that the typeface is readable for everyone, and that there is a good amount of space between lines and blocks of type, and on the page in general, you're making a very good start!

- A very useful guide to web typefaces (Motive, 2008): www.motive.co.nz/guides/typography/webfonts.php

- Vassar—nice explanation of web typefaces (Brown, 2003): http://adminstaff.vassar.edu/tibrown/thesis/screenfaces.html

- "Typefaces—Web Style Guide" (Lynch & Horton, 2009): http://webstyleguide.com/wsg3/8-typography/4-web-typefaces.html

- "Visual Design—Web Style Guide" (Lynch & Horton, 2009): http://webstyleguide.com/wsg3/7-page-design/3-visual-design.html

- "Design Simply—Access by Design" (Lynch & Horton, 2009): http://universalusability.com/access_by_design/fundamentals/simply.html

Reflection

While websites are more complex and visual than online courses, they are online and, as such, can help you review some basic principles of online design. Compare the following sets of competitive websites in terms of the design principles laid out here and the use of media covered in the chapter. Your main concern in reviewing them is usability:

- What is the purpose of the website?

- Is it easy to sort out—can you find what you need?

- Is all the text easily readable?

- Is it attractive—do you want to be there?

Compare the following with each other within these sets:

- www.aol.com, www.bing.com, www.google.com, www.yahoo.com

- www.guardianweekly.co.uk, www.nytimes.com, www.time.com

- www.apple.com, www.dell.com, www.hp.com

- www.adobe.com, www.microsoft.com, www.oracle.com

- www.arts.ac.uk, www.fitnyc.edu, www.fullsail.edu, www.nas.edu.au, www.ocad.ca

- www.hbs.edu, www.london.edu, www.wharton.upenn.edu

You can do more comparisons in areas that interest you.

4.7 Summary and Standards

Using the standards of good, clear visual design elements can just become habit if you pay attention to them in the early stages of writing.

Again, the focus here is on simplicity, clarity, and openness. There should be nothing in the design of the page that distracts from communication. On the contrary, an open, clear, attractive page design enhances communication.

Look at Figures 4.3 and 4.4 again. Although visual enhancements have been added, none of this distracts or detracts. White space, bold and italic fonts, and different typefaces and type sizes are used purposefully to make distinctions, emphasize, and enhance readability, comprehension, and learning.

Layout

☐ Page layout is uncluttered and open, and includes a significant amount of white space.

☐ There is sufficient space between lines, paragraphs, and to the right and left of text so that it stands out and is easy to read.

☐ Text is left-justified and right margins are ragged.

Text

☐ Headings and subheadings are used consistently to logically organize content.

☐ A universal sans serif web typeface (e.g. Verdana) assures access across platforms and enhances screen readability.

☐ Type size should be large enough to be easily readable by all students.

☐ Bold and italic typefaces are used sparingly only to emphasize important items.

☐ Underlining is used only for hyperlinks.

☐ Words in all caps are avoided.

Color

☐ Color is used with purpose.

☐ There is good contrast between text and background.

Graphic Elements

☐ Visual elements (e.g. icons, shading, and color) are used consistently to distinguish between different types of course elements (e.g. lessons, assignments, audio, and video).

☐ Use bullets or numbers to set apart items that can be listed.

☐ Numbers are used to identify sequential steps in a task or process. They are also used for rankings and setting priorities.

☐ Bullets are used to highlight a series of items that are not prioritized or sequential.

Chapter 5

Engaging the Online Learner

Knowledge is to be acquired only by a corresponding experience. How can we know what we are told merely?

Henry David Thoreau

Learning is not a spectator sport. Students do not learn much just by sitting in classes listening to teachers, memorizing pre-packaged assignments and spitting out answers. They must talk about what they are learning, write about it, relate it to past experiences and apply it to their daily lives. They must make what they learn part of themselves.

Chickering & Gamson (1987)

Three nights a week, Paul comes home from work, eats, then goes to sit alone in front of his computer. He stares at the screen, slowly scrolling and reading through the dense text. The "lecture" was written by a teacher hundreds of miles away. Paul studies online because this is the only way he can finish his degree and move on to better work opportunities.

Although he has contact with the teacher and the students through typewritten online discussions, these, like the teacher's "lectures," are long and tedious. He finds studying online an isolating experience, and it all takes more time than he counted on. Sometimes, he thinks he will just drop out, but his desire to improve his life keeps him motivated, so he carries on in spite of the mental drudgery.

Paul's teacher is required to teach this course online. She has done her best to recreate her lectures in written form, but just feels that it's not the same. There is no spontaneity. It can be challenging to make the subject matter interesting in a classroom setting, but online it just doesn't seem to work at all. She misses the contact with the students. The typewritten discussions just go on and on. She doesn't feel good about the experience in general. Her dropout rate is higher online.

The story above presents the classic negative image of online teaching and learning. We are here to tell you that online learning can be involving, interesting, interactive, and social—in other words, engaging.

Note: Any time you need a reference point for an online course or learning management system, refer to the Chapter 2 tour for a complete example.

5.1 Teaching Components

There are essentially three components to online teaching (see Figure 5.1).

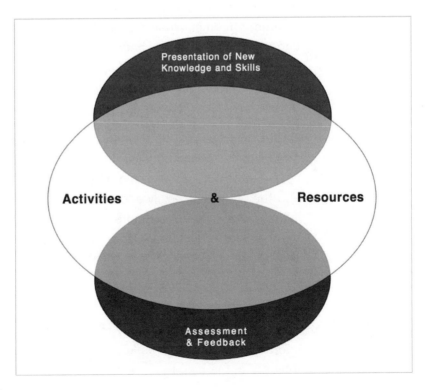

Figure 5.1
Three components to online teaching

The presentation of new knowledge and skills is the portion of the online course dedicated to introducing students to new topics. The activities and resources you construct are structured opportunities for students to practice and apply new knowledge and skills. Assessment of activities or other means is the point where the teacher (and possibly peers) provide feedback on student learning. All of these components can and should be engaging. **Active and engaging online courses are**:

- **Clearly and attractively presented**. The material is inviting and openly displayed. There are no barriers to understanding. A variety of different modes (e.g. audio, text, video, images, hands-on) for presentations and activities capture the interest and imaginations of learners.

- **Active and hands-on**. The material requires that learners are not only reading, listening, or watching, but doing something.

- **Authentic and meaningful**. The material is real, and/or comes close to real-world circumstances. It is true to its desired outcome. When a skill is being taught, learners can see the relationship between what they are doing in the course and its real-world application. Thus, the material is meaningful, motivating, and, potentially, even inspiring to both student and teacher.

- **Collaborative**. Learning is seen as a social experience. The learners feel responsible for their own learning. They contribute to others' learning. Contact with other learners and the teacher is easily accessible and continual. The learning environment promotes cooperation and sharing of perspectives. This leads students to develop multiple viewpoints and think critically. This also creates community.

- **Reflective**. The material encourages self-observation. There is time and opportunity to reflect built into the course. Self-assessments keep learners tuned in to where they are in the learning process.

- **Responsive to a variety of learning styles.** For example, there is recognition of the learning preferences of intrapersonal learners, as well as interpersonal learners (see Figure 5.2). Hands-on, visual, logical, and linguistic learners are all considered.

We will look at the qualities of engaged learning in more detail as we move through the development of the components that make up an online course.

5.2   Learning Styles

> [O]nce we realize that people have very different kinds of minds, different kinds of strengths—some people are good in thinking spatially, some in thinking language, others are very logical, other people need to be hands on and explore actively and try things out—then education, which treats everybody the same way, is actually the most unfair education. Because it picks out one kind of mind, which I call the law professor mind— somebody who's very linguistic and logical—and says, if you think like that, great, if you don't think like that, there's no room on the train for you.
>
> Edutopia (1997), interview with Howard Gardner

A brief article on Gardner's work with multiple intelligences with links: www.infed.org/ thinkers/gardner. htm.

Howard Gardner, a Harvard University education professor published his landmark book, *Frames of Mind: The Theory Of Multiple Intelligences*, in 1983. Gardner's work has resonated with many educators. It was an exciting revelation and has transformed what we know about learning. While many college and adult educators embrace the concept of addressing learning styles, many fewer do it than should. Both this book and the book's website model an approach that focuses on a variety of learning styles.

When following a purely textual model, online study emphasizes only linguistic intelligence. Visual learners, for example, need visual content to do their best.

Relatively speaking, it's easier to incorporate a variety of media into an online learning environment than an onsite class. Access to the technology that facilitates this is a given. This not only makes the course more engaging for all learners but

An *intra*personal learner:

- needs to spend time alone to think and reflect

- is strong-willed and independent

- thinks about life and the future

- keeps a personal journal

- is self-employed or would like to be

- can spend days at a time alone

An *inter*personal learner:

- is thought of as a good advisor

- prefers to talk out problems and work with others rather than alone

- enjoys teaching others

- feels comfortable in a crowd

- prefers playing games with others rather than alone

Figure 5.2
A comparison of interpersonal and intrapersonal learners

also pays attention to the needs of those with visual, logical (charts, diagrams), and musical (audio) learning styles.

Some learners need active, hands-on engagement to do their best. Emphasizing engaged learning especially supports learners in this area.

Online learning can be a rather solitary experience, perhaps appealing to the intrapersonal learner. Planning for collaboration and active learning, and incorporating outside resources addresses interpersonal and kinesthetic (hands-on/physically engaged) learning.

 Presentations of new knowledge and skills, activities, and assessments address a variety of learning styles.

5.3 Roles of Participants in an Engaged Learning Process

Online course activities are more engaging when both teacher and learner participate in the learning process.

Teacher's Role

The teacher is just as engaged as the learners in online activities. She guides learners through the process of

The VARK questionnaire— http://vark-learn. com/english

discovery, understanding, and knowledge construction. As facilitator and/or guide, the teacher helps learners to recognize their goals and work toward achieving them. Students bring in new information and experiences alongside the teacher. She often finds that she is learning alongside the learners.

 The teacher is a participant in the learning process.

Reflection

The chances are a learner will not be a linguistic or visual learner per se, but they will be stronger in some learning styles than others.

Why not take the VARK test? While it doesn't cover all of Gardner's intelligences, it will give you a good idea of how his ideas play out.

Once you have a sense of your strongest learning styles, look at some websites. Which address your learning style? Which do not? How does the design of websites affect your attitude and willingness to spend time visiting them?

Now, look through this book and its website. We have tried to address a variety of learning styles. Are you comfortable with the way the content is presented? Imagine you are someone with a complementary learning style to yours. Do you think they would be comfortable with the way information is presented? What have we done to make this information appeal to a range of learning styles? What haven't we done? How does this relate to online learning?

The Role of the Learner

Engaged learners are active participants in the learning process. They are responsible for their own learning and frequently contribute to others' learning. As active participants, learners explore, and are encouraged to construct, their own understandings of knowledge. They interact with the material, the technology, real-world situations, and others in the course to develop their understandings. The specific roles will change depending upon whether they are working alone, in pairs, in groups, or as a class.

 Learners take responsibility for their learning and, at times, the learning of others.

Active learning simply means the learners are "doing." Doing includes writing, discussing, asking, questioning, critiquing, and collaborating. For more detail, refer to the use of verbs in the learning outcomes in Appendix A.

The Role of the Learner as a Member of a Group

Learning is a social process (Dewey, 1997 [1938]); learners are in a class with others, including peers and teachers. Grouping learners together facilitates the sharing of multiple viewpoints and perspectives. Group members may present different viewpoints that reflect background (cultural, geographic, ethnic, socioeconomic), belief (political, religious), and/or experiences (professional, community, educational), which may influence others' perspectives and thinking. The group setting challenges learners to think beyond themselves and their subjective understandings of the world. Roles change according to how people work. Roles will also change depending upon the part you play (e.g. mediator, organizer, recorder, researcher, presenter, etc.).

The Role of the Learner Working in Pairs

Pairing learners is another form of grouping, where the exchanges between two learners are more effective than they would be in a group setting. Learners may work in pairs for specific types of assignments. In certain learning skills (e.g., languages, math, writing) areas, they can reinforce each other's work more efficiently than when working in a larger group. When pairing learners, they should be switched off more frequently than in the group setting, so they are exposed to a range of skills and knowledge levels.

The Role of the Learner Working Alone

The intrapersonal learner needs to have the opportunity to work alone. This type of learner is engaged through activities that can be completed independently. Give learners the opportunity to work alone once in awhile.

The Role of the Learner as a Member of a Community

Finally, the learner has a role as a member of the class community, relating to the class as a whole, as well as to the teacher. These roles are supported through development of content in a variety of formats. Class participation in discussion forums plays the dominant role in providing learner-to-class interaction.

☑ Class participation activities (e.g. discussion boards, wikis, social networks) are used to encourage collaboration.

Personal Perspective

Scott Thornbury

Experience has taught me that I teach better when I am also learning. For example, I'm a better language teacher when I'm also a language learner. And I'm a better teacher trainer when I, in turn, am learning a new skill.

Hence, my three years' experience working on the online program at The New School has been extraordinarily formative—the experience of learning how to exploit the available technologies in order to create a vibrant learning community has, I think, informed and improved my teaching—not just in this program, but whenever I have to face a new group of learners. I hope my students share some of this excitement!

Scott Thornbury lives in Barcelona. He designed and teaches two courses in the MA in Teaching English to Speakers of Other Languages at The New School in New York City.

Scott's examples in this book come from a course on Language Analysis for Teachers: Phonology/Lexis/Syntax (first taught at The New School). The textbook Scott uses, his own *About Language*, provides most of the activities for the course. To complement this, his online learners spend a fair amount of time working through online, interactive presentations that introduce, support, and reinforce the content.

5.4　Collaborative Learning

Communication and collaboration with others support active and engaged learning. Collaborative group work is learner-centered. It requires that all members of the group actively participate. They are then responsible for their own learning and, in part, the learning of others.

Collaboration encourages the sharing of information and perspectives, and requires both independent responsibility and cooperation. For example, a learner may be required to work as a member of a team, or in pairs. In many cases, collaboration reflects the realities of working under real world conditions, where individuals may typically work in teams.

☑ **There are sufficient opportunities for learners to work collaboratively.**

Grouping Learners

Learners are encouraged to interact with others (fellow classmates, guests, the instructor, and outside sources) and benefit from their experience and expertise (see also Group Projects in 6.5).

Different types of activities require different ways to group learners. Here are four common grouping techniques:

1. **Heterogeneous groups**. Learners are grouped by their differences in skills and/or knowledge. For example, each learner in the group may have a different skill critical to the success of the group activity.

2. **Homogeneous groups**. Learners are grouped by their similarities in knowledge, skills, or simply by the group's unique task. For example, if you wanted to hold an online debate for or against an issue, the two sides should be fairly well matched.

For more details on how jigsaw groups work, see www. jigsaw.org.

3. **Jigsaw groups**. The jigsaw method is commonly used to have learners work cooperatively. Each group member is assigned a unique task. The goal is for the learners to

present their findings to one another. To ensure the findings are accurate, learners consult with members of other groups assigned with the same task.

4. **Pairs**. Learners are paired to work together on an activity. The instructor can pair the learners, or the learners can self-select. Note: Pairs only work if there is an even number of learners in the course.

The point is that you probably want to group learners in a thoughtful and appropriate way that draws upon the experience, knowledge, and skills of the students, rather than just randomly.

Preparing for Collaboration

When designing and planning for collaborative learning in your course:

- Create a safe and supportive culture.

- Provide guidelines and expectations for group activities.

- Indicate the responsibilities and roles of the students.

- Build in a way for learners to assess one another's performance working in the group.

Review the strategies for grouping learners for collaborative activities. Begin thinking about the following:

- Which of the following groupings is most appropriate for the subject area you are teaching:
    - small groups, 3–4?
    - large groups, 6–8?
    - whole class?
    - pairs?
    - individuals?

- Think about how to group students (see page 76).

- What is the teacher's role?

- What will be the product or outcome of their work?

☑ Students are encouraged to share resources as is appropriate.

☑ Learners are encouraged to interact with others (fellow classmates, course guests, etc.) and benefit from their experience and expertise.

☑ Collaborative activities are designed to facilitate a safe learning environment.

☑ Procedures for group activities are specified so that students are aware of their role and responsibility in collaborative activities.

Personal Perspective
Kristen Sosulski

I assign a lot of group work in my online courses. I teach professional fields so it's important to situate learners in authentic situations. Students studying online can benefit from working together in teams. Real work situations require collaboration across sites. Online is great for simulating offsite collaboration.

While my students may be studying abroad or in New York City, I like to provide them with tools for team collaboration. I particularly encourage (but never require) online real-time meetings for online teams. Some of the tools I recommend are Skype, Adobe Connect, Wimba Live Classroom, Google Chat, and Google Docs.

I also encourage my students to pick the collaboration tool of their choice for real-time or asynchronous meetings.

5.5 Summary and Standards

In this chapter we have introduced you to the key characteristics of engaged learning. It's simple really—when both teacher and learner collaborate in the learning process, online activities are more engaging.

Learning Styles

☐ Presentations of new knowledge and skills, activities, and assessments address a variety of learning styles.

Roles of the Participants in the Engaged Learning Process

☐ The teacher is a participant in the learning process.

☐ Learners take responsibility for their learning and, at times, the learning of others.

☐ Class participation activities (e.g. discussion boards, wikis, social networks) are used to encourage collaboration.

☐ Learners are encouraged to interact with others (fellow classmates, course guests, etc.) and benefit from their experience and expertise.

Collaborative Learning

☐ There are sufficient opportunities for learners to work collaboratively.

☐ Students are encouraged to share resources as is appropriate.

Preparing for Collaboration

☐ Collaborative activities are designed to facilitate a safe learning environment.

☐ Procedures for group activities are specified so that students are aware of their role and responsibility in collaborative activities.

Chapter 6 Activities and Tools: Working Collaboratively and Independently

This chapter introduces an essential collection of adaptable activities that can be used across a range of fields and types of students. What can be done with this collection is limited only by the imagination, experience, and problem-solving skills of the teacher/designer.

Above all, activities must support the learning outcomes of the course. The quality of the learning experience depends on what activities you use, and how engaging the activities are for the students.

We cover **six basic online activities** that work well across a range of subjects (see Table 6.1). Most experienced teachers have come up with a repertoire of activity setups that either fit into the activities we have discussed or can just be redesigned for an online course.

These activity types and variations are designed to address thinking skills and encourage active learning, collaboration, and class communication. We'll begin with the productive activities, then reflective activities, and finally introduce some examples of receptive activities.

☑ Activities are frequent and varied. Students may respond to questions, select options, provide information, or interact with others.

☑ Activities engage students in higher-level thinking skills, including critical and creative thinking, analysis, and problem solving.

☑ Activities encourage active interactions that involve course content and personal communication.

☑ Resources and activities support learning outcomes.

Table 6.1 Online activity types and tools

Type of Activity	Tool	Variation	Participants
Class discussion	Discussion forum	• building a class community • question and answers • weekly topic discussions	pairs to full class
Journal writing	Blog	• individual reflections • teacher reflections/modeling	individuals
Shared knowledge base	Wiki	• collaborative glossary • annotated bibliography	group to class
Practice exercises	Testing/Quizzing	• multiple-choice • self-assessment	individuals to pairs
Projects	Multiple options such as workgroups, wikis, blogs, or discussion forums	• group project presentations • group research projects	individuals to pairs to class
Receptive activities	PDFs, podcasts, YouTube, Google Presentations, etc.	• teacher/student audio/visual presentations • course readings • miscellaneous audios and videos	individuals

6.1   Class Participation and Discussions

Online class discussions facilitate student–class participation in an online course.

Types of Discussion Activities

There are many ways to create dynamic and rich class discussions in an online course. Shaul (2007) identifies three discussion forum types:

- social
- general, and
- topic-driven.

For each type, the goal is to create a space that encourages discussion and community. Three small discussion activities are presented below. We encourage you to use all three when designing the course.

Discussion Board

Online Class Discussion

What Happens?

Online discussions in an asynchronous environment are set up as written "conversations" between two class members to the entire class. See Figure 6.1 for an example of a simple discussion forum called "Introduce Yourself."

The content and goals of your activity dictate the appropriate configuration. You can easily upload images, link to websites, and embed audio and video segments in your discussion posts.

Why?

Discussion is a core activity in any class, online or onsite. Very often the discussion forum is the central place where class members get together to communicate. It is often at the core of the learning process and participation is usually required at least 2 to 3 times a week.

Where Does It Happen?

All LMSs provide a communication tool for discussion, known as a discussion forum, a forum, a discussion board, or a bulletin board. Discussion forums vary in their design, functionality and setup; however, they all have certain characteristics in common.

Who?

Pairs to whole class including the teacher.

How?

The teacher sets up the topic by **creating a forum in the discussion board**. This may be a question to the class or a topic for conversation (e.g. Introduce Yourself, Q&A, etc.). **Each forum has a topic title and topic posting** (see Figure 6.1).

Learners reply to the forum topic posed by the teacher. Each reply (thread) contains a subject related to the topic, and a message (the response). The student's subject may be Vanessa's Introduction (see Figure 6.2). The message is the actual student introduction written in text form.

Class members (both students and teacher) reply to each other's threads. See the reply in Figure 6.3.

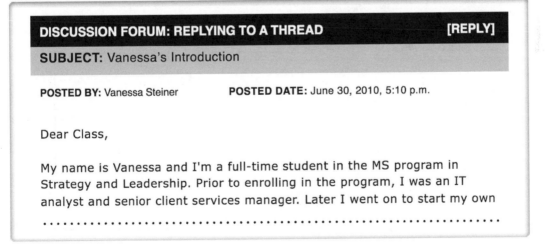

DISCUSSION FORUM [REPLY]

TOPIC: Introduce Yourself **POSTED DATE**: 6/29/2010, 1:00 PM

Welcome to Collaboration Technologies!

In this course we will be working together collaboratively to achieve the course objectives throughout the semester. I look forward to getting to know you over the course of the semester. To get things started, please introduce yourself to your classmates. You can do that by **adding a thread** to this **discussion forum**. In your reply, tell us a little about yourself and what you hope to achieve in this course.

Best,
Professor Sosulski

+ **RE: Vanessa's Introduction**
        Posted by Vanessa Steiner, Student – Posted on 3/30/2010, 5:10 PM

  + **RE: RE: Vanessa's Introduction**
          Posted by Kristen Sosulski, Faculty – Posted on 3/30/2010, 6:18 PM

+ **RE: James' Introduction**
        Posted by James Jacobs, Student – Posted on 3/30/2010, 7:57 PM

Figure 6.1 An example of a threaded discussion forum from Kristen's course, prompting class members to post an introduction of themselves

DISCUSSION FORUM: REPLYING TO A THREAD [REPLY]

SUBJECT: Vanessa's Introduction

POSTED BY: Vanessa Steiner **POSTED DATE:** June 30, 2010, 5:10 p.m.

Dear Class,

My name is Vanessa and I'm a full-time student in the MS program in Strategy and Leadership. Prior to enrolling in the program, I was an IT analyst and senior client services manager. Later I went on to start my own

Figure 6.2 A reply posted by a student introducing herself to the class

Activity: Social Forums—Building a Class Community

During the early part of an online course, it is critical for class members to get to know one another, and begin to build an online class community.

The teacher also participates in the online activity. For example, the teacher can also post her introduction as a thread. Of course, she will respond to the students' threads as they unfold.

Below are some ideas for topics that encourage rapport building:

- Class introductions and ice-breaking tasks (see Figures 6.1, 6.2, and 6.3).

- Geography. Students can group themselves by their location to arrange "face-to-face" or online "real-time" meetings. They can then report back to the class as a whole.

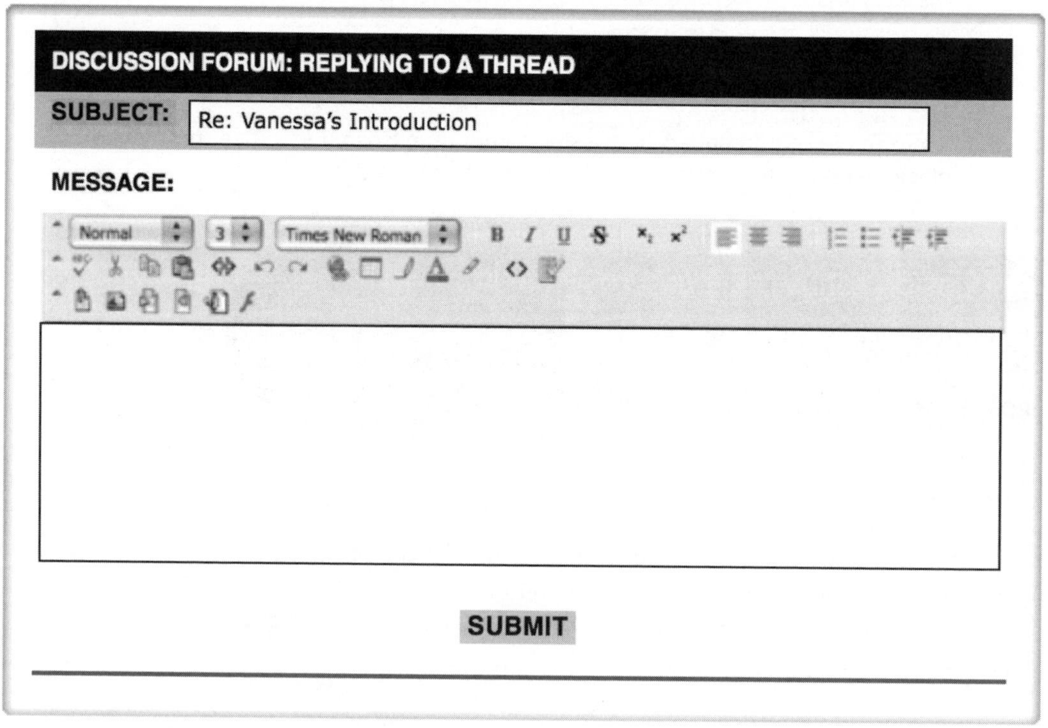

DISCUSSION FORUM: REPLYING TO A THREAD

SUBJECT: Re: Vanessa's Introduction

MESSAGE:

| Normal | 3 | Times New Roman | B *I* U S |

SUBMIT

Figure 6.3 The reply message window

- Online "class cafe." This is an open, ongoing forum where students talk with classmates. They share topics of interest such as recent news articles, career opportunities, etc. This is similar to students meeting in a real cafe during course breaks.

 An online space (e.g. discussion board, social network) is in place for students to meet outside the class.

Discussion Board—Variation

Online Class Discussion—Introduce Yourself

The "Introduce Yourself" discussion forum has the following advantages in an online course. It:

- allows the teacher and learners to get to know one another and possibly extend their relationships into another social forum such as the class cafe

- provides an introduction and practices on using the forums in the online course, and

- enables the teacher to identify learners with similar interests, which may inform how the teacher groups learners for collaborative work later on in the course.

Return to Figure 6.1 for an example of creating an introductory activity where all students introduce themselves and share their interests.

Activity: General Forums—Ice-breaker

An ice-breaker should not require anything more than the ability to express knowledge of self. It relates more to the personal life than to the academic life of the learner.

Conrad & Donaldson (2004: 47)

Salmon (2002), in her book *eTivities*, provides examples of online ice-breakers. Our favorite examples include a "Quiz of all the class members."

In this ice-breaker the teacher asks all the students to post some information about themselves. After each student has contributed, the teacher can set up a quiz that tests the students' knowledge of each class member. See Figure 6.4 for an example of the first part of the ice-breaker activity. After students post their biography to the discussion forum, they are directed to read the biographies of the other students. Finally, students take an online quiz that is set up more like a contest to test their knowledge of their fellow classmates. The highest scorer is rewarded with a prize. A prize might be extra credit on an assignment.

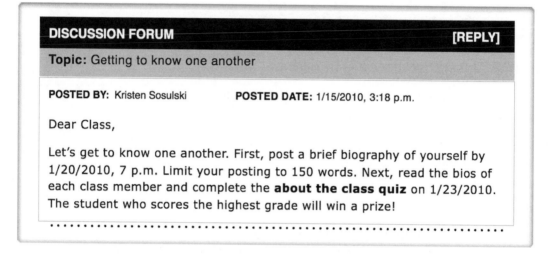

DISCUSSION FORUM [REPLY]

Topic: Getting to know one another

POSTED BY: Kristen Sosulski   **POSTED DATE:** 1/15/2010, 3:18 p.m.

Dear Class,

Let's get to know one another. First, post a brief biography of yourself by 1/20/2010, 7 p.m. Limit your posting to 150 words. Next, read the bios of each class member and complete the **about the class quiz** on 1/23/2010. The student who scores the highest grade will win a prize!

Figure 6.4 An online ice-breaker (adapted from Salmon, 2002)

Activity: General Forums—Question and Answer (Q&A)

Tip
For a Q&A to be successful, the teacher should encourage the class to respond to each other's questions. This can save the teacher and students time.

When online learners have a question, there are two ways to have them ask it:

- Email the question directly to the teacher as a private communication.

- Post the question in a discussion forum as a public communication to the class.

The drawback of the email approach is that the learner is relying on the teacher as the sole provider of information. Instead, set up a Q&A discussion forum for the duration of the online course (see Figure 6.5). This saves time for the teacher and encourages communication. Be sure to include this in your communication strategy in your syllabus (see Chapter 9).

TOPIC: Questions and Answers   **POSTED DATE:** 1/26/2010, 9:07 a.m.

The purpose of this forum is for you have a place to ask course-related questions throughout the semester. I'll do my best to answer your questions. When appropriate, please feel free to post your thoughts to questions posed by others as well.

Professor Gaynor

SUBJECT: APA and Required Readings
Posted by Steven Manis, Student -- Posted on 1/26/2010, 11:40 a.m.

Hi Professor Gaynor,

I have two questions. First, the first assignment requires that I write my paper in APA style. Can you point me to a online resource that will provide me with

Figure 6.5 A Q&A discussion forum

Discussion Board—Variation

Online Class Discussion—Question and Answer

In an online course, the Q&A discussion forum has the following advantages:

- It provides a single, convenient place for learners to ask administrative questions related to assignments, due dates, and requirements.

- A student's questions are made public to the class. This is similar to a student raising her hand in an onsite class. Everyone gets to see the question. The teacher has to respond only once to the question and all students will benefit from learning the new information the response provides.

- It encourages community-building within the course. Students are encouraged to help others by posting their thoughts on the question. This supports a student-centered approach.

Figure 6.5 is an example of a Q&A discussion forum. Notice how the teacher keeps the purpose of the forum brief and encourages other learners to respond when they feel it is appropriate.

Online Class Discussion—Content discussions

The "content-based discussion forum" has the following characteristics. It:

- provides a place for asking questions about and discussing a new topic

- designates a place for learners to explore the topic with others and clarify their understanding of the weekly course content

- enables students to analyze and synthesize class readings and observations through a focused exchange of ideas.

Figure 6.6 is an example of a topic-based discussion. Notice how the students are replying to one another, not just to the teacher.

Activity: Topic-driven Forums—Weekly Content Discussions

Tip

Be sure that the questions you pose to students inspire conversation and discussion. Avoid yes/no questions and those that can be answered with only one or two words.

As discussed throughout this book, class participation is critical in an online class. Topic-driven forums encourage and facilitate discussion of salient course topics. These forums focus on a single topic for a defined period of time.

Weekly topic-based discussions are the equivalent of classroom discussions in an onsite class. Once forum content is presented, this is where the class goes to discuss it. Typically, student participation is tied to the class participation grade. This ensures active class participation (see Figure 6.6).

One of the benefits of this asynchronous discussion is that students can reflect and think about their responses rather than having to respond immediately, as is typical in an onsite class. Also, each and every student must respond. In an onsite class this is usually not the case.

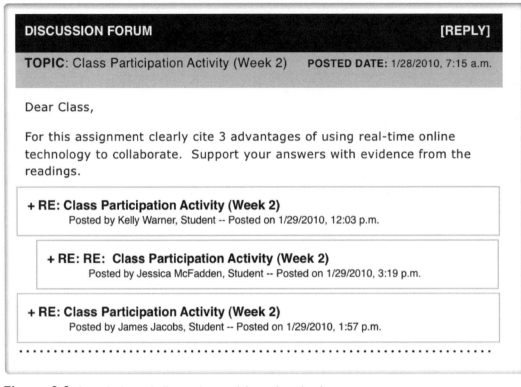

Figure 6.6 A topic-based discussion activity using the forum

6.2 Online Journaling Activities

Types of Online Journaling Activities

Tip

It's easy for students to post a response to the questions or topics posed by the teacher. Encourage students to reply to one another in your instructions and in the syllabus. Indicate that not doing so can affect their grade.

The variance in types of journals relates to what the teacher, as guide, emphasizes and what the student prefers. This has a great deal to do with who is reading the journal: one, a small group, or the whole class.

Students may not want to share reflective work with anyone but the teacher. When this is the case, what benefits the student most should determine the outcome. **The goal in this case is that the students develop the habit of reflecting on their work**. In order to do this, they must be comfortable with the process.

Tip

A simpler alternative (if you do not have access to a blog) allows students to post to a discussion forum instead. Set up a separate forum for each student. Create an online class rule in which only the "owner" of a forum can create threads and all others can reply (this is equivalent to commenting in a blog).

Activity: Individual Reflections via the Blog

In an online course, there are several ways for the teacher to assess how well students understand assigned readings. One technique is for students to complete a reading and then reflect upon it afterwards. Students can summarize their interpretation of the reading and relate it to prior knowledge and understanding (see Figure 6.9). While this often occurs in shared dialogue in the discussion board, journal writing may allow the students to express themselves more freely.

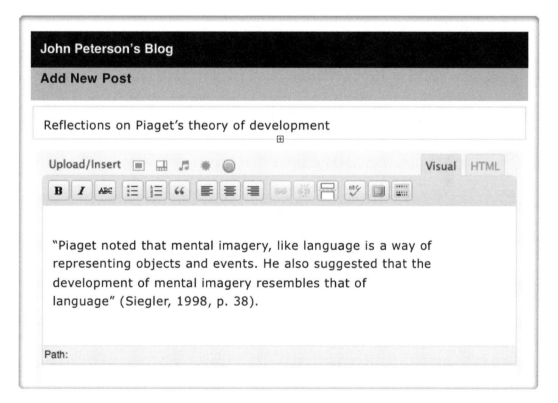

Figure 6.7 An entry on a blog

Online Journaling

What Happens?

The student keeps a log of written entries, organized chronologically by date or by topic. Similar to discussions forums, blogs are typically public (to the class) and, therefore, this is not a private activity. This allows the teacher (or the entire class) to view and comment on the student postings/entries throughout the course.

Why?

Online journaling is an activity that allows students to reflect on the steps they take to understand new knowledge or develop a new skill. This reflection can take many forms, such as critiquing class readings or logging progress on a project or research paper. Journaling is an individual activity that lets the teacher know what students are thinking about their own learning and development.

Where does it happen?

In a Blog. A blog is short for weblog, or more simply, a running web page with multiple entries (articles, reflections, diary entries, etc.) that includes text, images, links to websites, audio, and/or video clips. Some LMSs have blogging as an option. If yours doesn't, try these popular blogging platforms: Blogger, LiveJournal, Typepad, Movable Type, and WordPress.

Who?

Individuals blogging with one or more class members reading and responding.

How?

- **The teacher introduces the assignment**. The instructions include the teacher's assessment criteria for the blog posting and comments).

- **The student posts an entry to his/her blog**. The student keeps a log of written entries, organized chronologically by date or by topic. An entry is simply written text that may include images, video, and/or hyperlinks (see Figure 6.7).

- **The class members including the teacher leave comments** on each author's blog (see Figure 6.8).

- **The blog author may also post comments back** to his/her own blog.

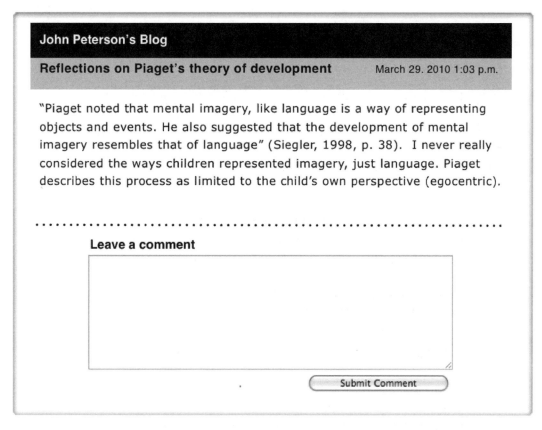

John Peterson's Blog

Reflections on Piaget's theory of development   March 29. 2010 1:03 p.m.

"Piaget noted that mental imagery, like language is a way of representing objects and events. He also suggested that the development of mental imagery resembles that of language" (Siegler, 1998, p. 38). I never really considered the ways children represented imagery, just language. Piaget describes this process as limited to the child's own perspective (egocentric).

· ·

Leave a comment

(Submit Comment)

Figure 6.8 Adding a comment to a blog posting

Journaling—Variation

Teacher Reflections

W

See the website for another take on using the blog as a place to post individual reflections.

Teachers share their reflections with the class and solicit comments. The teacher also serves as a model.

This is a great example of the teacher as a participant in the online course. This includes the main posting by the teacher and the comments/responses by students that are appended to the blog posting.

Individual Reflections

In an online course, individual reflections via the blog have the following characteristics. They:

- provide a space for regular running reflection on readings;

- reinforce the course readings and connect them to the learner's prior knowledge

- help the students self-identify questions in areas where they need to clarify their understanding (Palloff & Pratt, 2005).

Figure 6.9 is an example of a student's blog posting from Steven Goss's Narrative and Dynamic Structures course at NYU-SCPS. **Take note of the blog comments**. These are appended to the actual blog posting. Notice the conversation that is taking place between the student and teacher.

Simulation as narrative enabler?

Blog posted by Andrew Wilson

... Narrative would be created by the author, perhaps (to get players going), but also by players. Evoked, enacted, and environmental narratives are all possible, and emergent narratives would surface—particularly in the conflict between griefers and performers.

Some kind of statistics system could encourage achievers to create compelling narratives. Here, at Frasca's third level, incentive could be given to create various kinds of narratives, to participate in them or add to them.

I wonder about how this compares to Second Life. Is there much story telling there, or is it more about social networking? How permanent are creations and can other people change them? I think others cannot—creators pay money, sometimes. Does the imposed economy there stifle innovation by segregating creative spaces?

Figure 6.9a A student's reflection on the course readings via the blog, with teacher comments below shown in Figure 6.9b

Reprinted with permission

Comment posted by Steven Goss on 3/23/2010 5:55 p.m.

I think you are describing what Lindley is trying to define with emergent narrative, which Jenkins also makes reference to, although his definition is not as focused on database concepts. Lindley appears to be almost describing an experience comparative to database narrative. See his reference to the Façade interactive drama system. With Jenkins, emergent narrative is more of a space where the player is able to engage in story making, such as with The Sims. I think when we cross into Second Life, we move away from simulation and narrative gaming and into Social Networking. It is less first or third person environments and more avatar making and communication.

This is not to say that gaming does not utilize Social Networking experience, in fact, Lindley would say it is a relevant experience for gaming. However, I may suggest there is a difference between making an avatar and playing a character. I am sure I just opened about 10 different threads to go down with that commentary, such as what is the line between avatar and character. However I think for this discussion we need to first figure out gaming before moving into narrative and social networking.

Figure 6.9b Teacher comments for the student's reflection shown in Figure 6.9a

Reprinted with permission

6.3   Shared Knowledge Base

Wikis are "flexible" and "intensely collaborative." They are "administered by a number of people" and can be "organized in innumerable ways." If you want to engage in personal reflection, you use a blog, but if you want collaboration, you use a wiki (Zeinstejer, 2008).

Note: Wikipedia (www.wikipedia.com) is an example of how a wiki is used to support the ongoing contributions to an online encyclopedia. Unlike a physical encyclopedia, a wiki encyclopedia is not a static set of information. As new events occur, they are added to Wikipedia from the large online community of contributors.

Types of Knowledge-Base Building Activities

- Online class glossary.

- Group research project.

- Online class bibliography and/or web resources relevant to course topics.

- Group or class projects—media, art, planning, writing, science, product development, etc.

- Error correction—language, facts, history, news, etc.

- Time lines, chronological lists.

- Annotated article, poem, case study, reading, etc. with multimedia and links.

- Group or class storyboards for film-, media-, and technology-related subjects.

Activity: Collaborative Glossary

When learners are taking a course in a new area of study that includes unfamiliar terminology, there are two ways to present information:

- the teacher defines it directly for the learner; or

- the learner identifies the terms he doesn't know and seeks out the definition.

What if the students created their own glossary?

Activity: Collaborative Timeline/Chronological List

To give students a big picture perspective, have them create a time line or chronological list on an area of study. The area of study may be a field itself such as: a scientific or mathematical discipline, higher education, a religion, a branch of philosophy, etc. Or something more specific such as milestones in the history of a movement including influences, developments and events that affected its evolution.

Shared Knowledge Base

What Happens?

The class/group is essentially building one or more documents together, online. Anyone who is given permission to work on the document can add, modify, and/or delete the contents. The authorship is shared. It is not just a reflection of one individual's participation and contribution. The content is always in progress and is thought of as growing and evolving.

Why?

Student collaboration builds community in an online class enabling the co-creation of knowledge and products, and aiding in the development of critical thinking skills (Palloff & Pratt, 2005). Additionally, collaborative projects emphasize to students that the online course is not just interacting with the teacher, but with their peers as well.

Where Does It Happen?

In a wiki—a collaborative tool in which an online document is created that supports the inclusion of text, images, video and audio, and links to other documents. Wikis are quick "because the process of reading and editing is combined" (Lamb, 2004). If your LMS doesn't have a wiki, some popular wikis include PBwiki and Wikispaces, or even Google Docs.

Who?

Group to class—the authorship of a wiki is shared. There can be groups of students working on different projects or the whole class working on one.

How?

* Teacher creates the wiki and enables the selected course members to edit it. Editing a wiki simply means adding to it and modifying it.

* Teacher posts instructions for the assignment within the wiki document.

* Students begin viewing, adding to, and modifying the content of the wiki.

Shared Knowledge Base

Variation—Collaborative Glossary

Building a shared online glossary has the following advantages in an online course. It:

- creates good study habits

- strengthens research skills

- leads to a better understanding of concepts through close-up work and analysis

- saves time for the teacher

- fosters collaboration skills

To create an online collaborative glossary, you can use a **wiki**. Figure 6.10 is an example of the activity description by Heidi Wittford in her graduate *Globalization and Higher Education* course at NYU. The activity begins with the teacher posting a term and its definition.

Note: This activity requires oversight and feedback from the teacher to ensure definitions provided are accurate.

Wiki Assignment

This wiki will be a repository for an ongoing list terms and definitions encountered in the readings and other course content. Since many of the terms encountered in the course content have multiple and contradictory definitions, keeping a running list will be helpful in sorting through complex and evolving definitions.

Figure 6.10 Teacher instructions for an online glossary-building activity

6.4 Practice Exercises

While many of the practice exercise types described below are not usually seen as collaborative, they are interactive. Under the right circumstances they can be a valuable addition to the work done in an online course. This is obviously true for certain kinds of skills classes such as languages and math.

Types of Practice Exercises

Multiple Choice

Learners select their answers based on a finite set of options. The questions may have answers that are mutually exclusive or not. The answers are evaluated by a computer and may include teacher-created feedback (see Figure 6.11).

Matching

The student matches an item in column A with an item in column B. The answers to matching question types can be evaluated on their computer (see Figure 6.12).

Fill-in-the-Blank

The student enters a word or a phrase to complete a statement (see Figure 6.13). The answers to fill-in-the-blank questions can be evaluated on their computer. However, **responses from students must be an exact match.** For example, a misspelling would count as a wrong answer.

Note: **This can be frustrating to the student and may impede learning** (e.g. in foreign languages). Use fill-in-the-blank exercises sparingly and with care when they are computer-corrected.

Practice Exercise

What Happens?

A testing and quizzing setup provides a channel for learners to practice with teacher-designed exercises and self-assessments. The teacher can address many levels of thinking skills through the use of multiple choice, matching, true/false, fill-in-the-blank, and short-answer questions.

Why?

The benefit of using the testing tool is the instant feedback it can provide to students.

Where Does It Happen?

Most LMSs are equipped with a **Test Manager**. This is a great tool for organizing exercises, despite its use of the word "test." It enables the teacher to set up a "test" with questions and provide students with feedback on correct and incorrect answers. See Figures 6.11–6.16 for standard question types available within an LMS-based Test Manager.

Who?

Individuals and pairs.

How?

1. Begin by drafting out the questions for the practice exercise.

2. Determine the grade percentage for the entire exercise and point value for each question.

3. Consider and craft the feedback that you would like to provide to students on their correct and incorrect answers, if any.

4. Build the test in the LMS.

5. Make the test available to the students and set the time frame, if relevant.

6. Direct students to the practice exercise.

7. Students go to the designated place in the online course to complete the practice exercises.

8. The teacher provides feedback to short-answer questions. The computer provides the teacher-created feedback on those questions that are multiple choice, true/false, fill-in-the-blank, and/or matching.

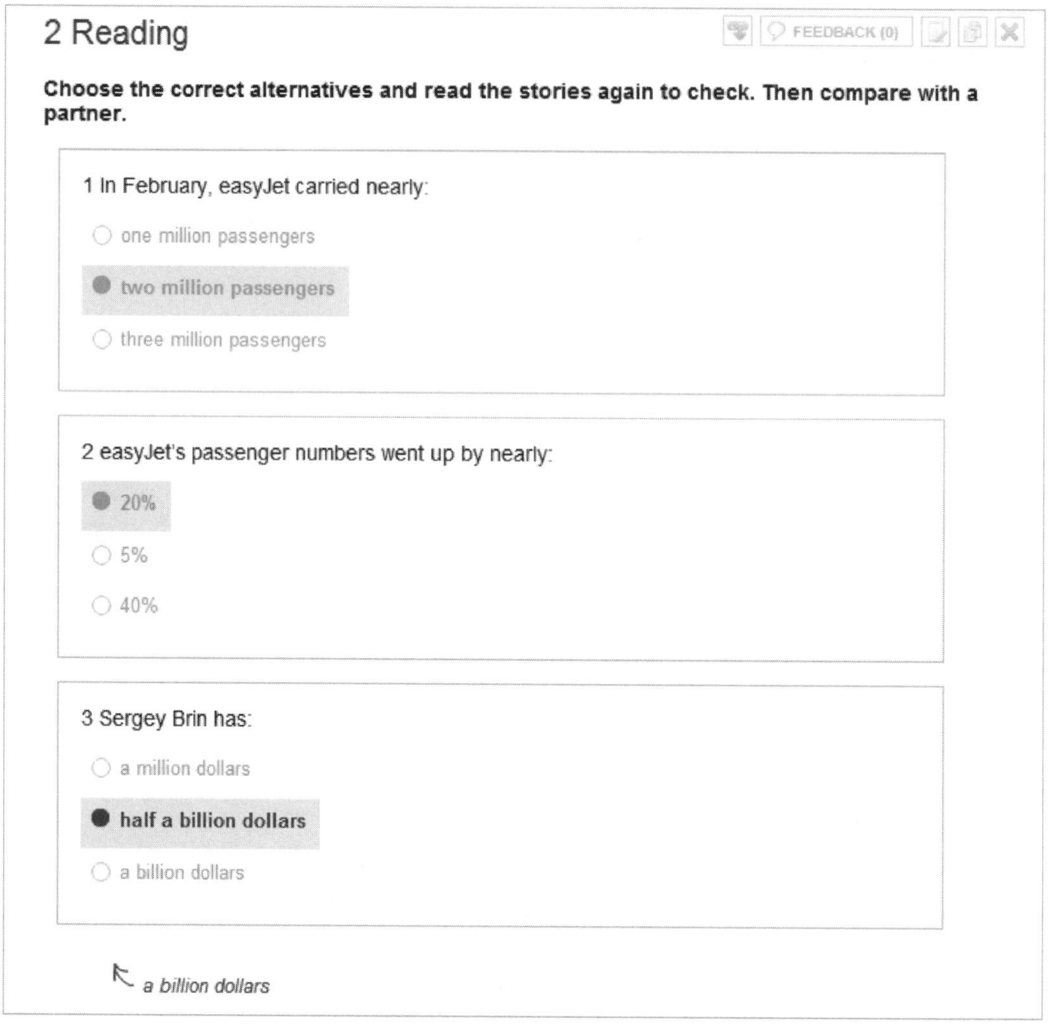

2 Reading

FEEDBACK (0)

Choose the correct alternatives and read the stories again to check. Then compare with a partner.

1 In February, easyJet carried nearly:

○ one million passengers

● **two million passengers**

○ three million passengers

2 easyJet's passenger numbers went up by nearly:

● **20%**

○ 5%

○ 40%

3 Sergey Brin has:

○ a million dollars

● **half a billion dollars**

○ a billion dollars

a billion dollars

Figure 6.11 A multiple-choice exercise with the correct answers highlighted and an incorrect answer highlighted and corrected

From Business Goals 3 (Student's Book) by Gareth Knight, Mark O'Neil, and Bernie Hayden, Unit 7 Business Media repurposed for online/blended delivery by English360. Reproduced with permission.

Figure 6.12

(Facing page: top) An online matching exercise with the correct and incorrect answers automatically corrected

Created by Emma Watson (English360) specifically for Marjorie Vai. Reproduced with permission.

Figure 6.13

(Facing page: bottom) An online fill-in-the-blank exercise with the correct and incorrect answers indicated

From Business Goals 3 (Student's Book) by Gareth Knight, Mark O'Neil, and Bernie Hayden, Unit 9 Part A Time Management. Repurposed for online/blended delivery by English360. Reproduced with permission.

Collocations

Trouvez la correspondance entre les deux parties de chaque phrase ci-dessous.

Click the grey areas to select matching items. Undo a match by clicking again.

assister à...	...un congrès ✓
embaucher...	...un nouvel employé ✓
fournir...	...des marchandises ✗
	↖ ...un service
fabriquer...	...un service ✗
	↖ ...des marchandises
réserver...	...une salle de conférence ✓

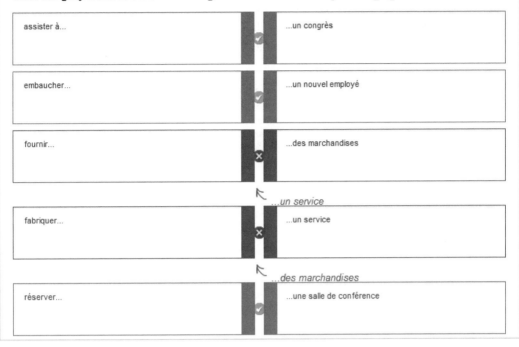

Harry:

Over the next three months, (1) **I will** ✗ *(the goal is to)* maintain sales of our services to current customers.

(2) **I'm going to** ✓ use the database to make a list of all the companies in my area... If I call them all next week, I can start visiting the following week. (3) **I plan to** ✓ visit all the companies in the next two months. (4) **If I** ✗ *(That way, I should)* have time after that to go back and revisit the companies which are undecided.

Ursula:

It's her job and she'll be much faster than you. (5) **That means you can** ✓ start calling your biggest customers...

Keep sending the information you collect back to Susana. (6) **If we don't** ✓ keep the database up-to-date, (7) **we'll** ✗ lose track of who you've visited and who you haven't visited. And one last thing: (8) **if you** ✓ divide up your area and concentrate your visits in smaller areas, (9) **you have to** ✗ *(you should)* find you're using your time more effectively...

True/False

The student evaluates whether a statement or phrase is true or false. The answers to true/false questions can be evaluated on their computer. These are similar in design to multiple-choice questions (see Figure 6.14).

---

7. Harry is a computer company executive, earning $200 per hour managing the company and promoting its products. His daughter Quinn is a high school student, earning $6 per hour helping her grandmother on the farm. Harry's computer is broken. He can repair it himself in one hour. Quinn can repair it in 10 hours. Harry's opportunity cost of repairing the computer is lower than Quinn's.

⊙ true

⊙ false

Figure 6.14

A true/false question type from Joelle Scally's Introduction to Macroeconomics course

Reprinted with permission

Compounding: You invest $5000 at an interest rate of 7%.

a) What is it worth in 1 year?
b) What is it worth in two years?
c) What is it worth in 10 years?

Please be sure to SHOW all formulas that you use, and any mathematical calculations that you use to get your answer in order to get partial credit.

Figure 6.15 An example of a short-answer question from a practice exercise given to new online teachers

Reprinted with permission

Drag and Drop

The student can manipulate phrases or objects by dragging them around the screen and then dropping them where they want (see Figure 6.16). This can be used for many of the above-mentioned purposes, but also has other uses such as having students categorize or organize items in defined ways.

Practice C

Patients pass from the care of one person to another several times on the way to surgery, and pre-operative information is checked by various staff members. Belinda is in the Operating Theatre holding area before she is taken in to have her operation performed.

Wendy, the Theatre Nurse, checks the patient details and details relating to the operation. She uses the green shaded area in the column marked O/T (Operating Theatre). Listen to the conversation. Which sections of the Checklist does Wendy double-check? Drag the sections into "Wendy double-checks" or "Wendy doesn't double-check".

▶ | 00:00 |

AUDIOSCRIPT

| Operation or procedure |

Wendy double-checks

Drop Here

| Operation site shaved |

| Pre-med given and signed for |

Wendy doesn't double-check

Drop Here

| Theatre gown worn / anti-embolic stockings / knickers |

| Nail varnish removed |

| Identify piercings |

| Name |

| Jewellery removed or taped |

| Any known allergies |

| ID bracelet |

Figure 6.16 An online drag-and-drop exercise

From Cambridge English for Nursing Intermediate Plus by Virginia Allum and Patricia McGarr, Unit 8 Charting and documentation: Pre-operative Checklist. Repurposed for online/blended delivery by English360. Reproduced with permission.

Feedback

Ideally, feedback that is generated automatically is descriptive in most subject areas. Explanations can accompany each answer and describe why the learner's selection was correct or incorrect. While designing and building the actual practice exercise is time-consuming, in the long run this can save the instructor time by automating feedback to students.

Note: **We recommend that practice exercises account for a small amount of the grade, if any.**

Activity: Self-assessment

Refer to Chapter 8 (see Figure 8.3 on page 142) for an example of an online self-assessment. Once students finish the self-assessment, they click on answers. A pop-up screen then appears with the answers.

 Go to the website for additional resources on practice activities.

Practice Exercise—Variation

Variation—Self-Assessment

Self-assessment activities have the following advantages in an online course. They:

- help students to pace their learning

- serve as a tool for learner reflection

- reinforce understandings because they are another form of built-in redundancy, and

- actively engage students in the course content and provide instantaneous feedback on their progress.

6.5   Group Projects

Types of Group Projects

There are many possibilities for group projects. We've highlighted two of the most common:

- an online presentation; and

- a research project/paper.

Activity: Online Group Presentation

There are many options for groups to make presentations. Presentations can be in the form of a pre-recorded video, a slide presentation that is narrated, a simple slide presentation with notes, or a combination of text, images, audio, and video.

Activity: Group Research Project/Paper

When introducing new course material, consider having learners discover and experience it rather than simply read about it. Small research projects can help learners construct their own understandings of a subject through various self-selected resources.

The project becomes more meaningful because the learners, rather than the teacher, select the resources and topics. Learners are responsible for their own learning. In discussions with the class (peers and teacher), the sharing of multiple viewpoints and perspectives occurs naturally. The teacher is more engaged because even she does not know everything that will be presented. She may learn something new as well.

☑ There are sufficient opportunities for learners to work collaboratively.

☑ Learners are encouraged to interact with others (fellow classmates, course guests, etc.) and benefit from their experience and expertise.

☑ Procedures for group activities are specified so that students are aware of their role and responsibility in collaborative activities.

Group Project

What Happens?

At the most basic level, students can communicate online privately with their group members and share basic word processing, presentation, and spreadsheet documents. The advantage is that each group can have its work stored in one place.

Why?

Collaborative and group work is learner-centered. It requires that group members actively participate. They are responsible for their own learning and, in part, the learning of others.

Where Does It Happen?

Workgroups are designated spaces within the LMS that enable two or more students to collaborate and communicate. Each team has its own workgroup space, accessible exclusively to that team and the instructor. Teams cannot see each other's work; however, the teacher can see the work of all teams.

The workgroup tool varies significantly from one LMS to another. Some offer robust communication tools such as private group discussion forums, drop boxes for file storage and sharing, group wikis, and group email.

Who?

Workgroups or groups.

How?

Organizing a group of students to work together on a project online requires the teacher to set up the necessary workspaces to facilitate the work, have clear requirements for individual participation in the group, and expectations of where the final projects is to be delivered (see also page 76, Grouping Learners).

To set up a group project the teacher needs to do the following:

1. Determine the team assignments. (Note: the teacher can only assign teams when the class begins. When planning, designing, and building the course, students have not yet begun the course; therefore, you must wait until the course officially begins.)
2. Create a workgroup space for each team.
3. Add the appropriate members to each team.
4. Notify the students of their team assignments via a course announcement and email them with clear instructions on how to access their team workgroup.

Group Project—Variation

Variation—Group Presentations

Table 6.2 shows a group project description for a team presentation. The students planned the presentation using communication and collaboration tools available to them within the workgroup.

Online group presentations have the following characteristics:

- Learners work together on a project and focus on communicating their findings in summary form.

- Presentations may include text, visuals, and multimedia, and hyperlinks to articulate products of the project work.

Group Project—Variation

Variation—Team Research Project

Effective online team research projects have the following characteristics.

They:

- situate students in an authentic context for conducting research using real tools and resources, such as online databases and library resources;

- guide students through the critical thinking process that moves students from novices towards being expert researchers; and

- allow the teacher and the groups to collaborate in the critique and assessment of research findings.

Table 6.2 An example of a group project/presentation

Group Project 3: Project Management and Industry Research

Learning outcomes

At the end of this project you will be able to:

- Develop a project plan with milestones, deliverables, and assigned tasks for this project using a project management collaborative tool, such as BaseCamp
- Critically compare and contrast collaboration technologies and the way they are used in a particular industry or sector
- Collaborate with an online team to develop a creative presentation

Description and Requirements

As a group, research the ways in which organizations in your assigned sector currently use technologies to collaborate in the workplace. Identify examples from reputable sources to support your presentation. These can include video, images, text, graphics, animations, diagrams, demonstrations, and charts. The group is encouraged to be creative with this presentation in terms of format and delivery.

Team industry/sector assignments:

- Team A—Research/Development
- Team B—Education
- Team C—Non profits/Philanthropy Groups
- Team D—Information/Communication Technology
- Team E—Creative/Media

The presentation must include the following:

- Team name and names of all team members
- Each team member's role and responsibilities using a responsibility chart
- A description of the team's assigned sector
- The types of group collaborative activities within the sector
- The resources used in the research
- The ways in which the team conducted the research
- At least ten model examples of the ways in which specific organizations within the team's assigned sector use technology for the collaborative activities (as identified in item 4)

Grading Criteria and Percentage

All seven topics are appropriately covered		70 Points
• Clearly articulated and well-designed presentation This includes consistent font style, color scheme, layout, readability, and creativity		15 Points
• The project plan and project management tool was followed and utilized appropriately		10 Points
• Presentation met all submission requirements and rules and was submitted on time		5 Points
	Total	100 Points

Due Date

3/25, by 11:59 p.m. EST

Submission Location

Project 3 Drop Box Folder

Table 6.3 Types of activities particularly suited to online courses

Activity Type	Activity Description
Problem-based learning	The activity presents a problem to be solved. The problem is genuine to the case or situation. The problem is presented within a realistic context. Learners have to actively apply their knowledge to solve the problem. The process is more important than the outcome (the answer). The problem may precede any lecture or presentation of new knowledge to the learner. It is the learner's role to determine what they need to learn to solve the problem.
Case study	Similar to problem-based learning, but presents a factually-based complex problem in which there is not necessarily a right or wrong answer. The case is usually read individually and discussed as part of a larger group (class/team).
Project-based learning	The outcome is as important as the process. The outcome is typically a product (e.g. website, work of art, creative writing, science experiments, blueprints, etc.).
Simulations	Approximate a real-life experience with many variables in which the learner is situated in a role. The student has to make many decisions that affect the outcome of her role in the simulated environment.
Simulator-based activities	Provides learners with an opportunity to experience something that is near to impossible to as a learner. This allows for failure without penalty (e.g. flying/crashing a plane, open-heart surgery). Simulators are used in the context of a larger activity, with goals, questions, etc.
Debates	A competitive activity that allows learners to apply their knowledge in the context of an argument. Usually done in teams.
Portfolio building	A collection of work amassed or collected over the duration of the course. This provides opportunities for learner reflection.
Critique	Engaging the students beyond whether they like or dislike something, with supporting evidence. Commonly used in art courses. This is great for critical thinking.
Primary research	An activity that involves gathering primary sources through interviews, questionnaires, and/or observation of events (e.g. research study).
Secondary research	An activity that involves reviewing secondary resources such as books, articles, etc. to create a literature review, annotated bibliography, etc.
Presentations	A demonstration of the learner's work summarized in a slide-show format, animation, video, audio, text, and/or a combination of these.
Practice exercises	A set of computer-graded questions (e.g. multiple choice, fill-in-the-blank, matching, true/false, etc.).
Receptive activities	Teacher audio/visual presentations and course readings. These are represented in course lessons as audio/video clips, pdf documents, and other presentation type formats such as PowerPoint and Google slide shows.

6.6 Summary and Standards

We introduced several types of activities that work well online. Refer to Table 6.3 (page 109) for a range of collaborative and individual activities. Many of these can also be used for class participation activities.

Now you have a basic understanding of a collection of activity environments than can be used for a wide range of involving and challenging learning experiences.

This collection offers many varied opportunities for learners to work collaboratively in groups. Learners are encouraged to interact with others (classmates, guests, the instructor, and outside resources), and benefit from others' experiences and expertise.

☐ Activities are frequent and varied. Students may respond to questions, select options, provide information, or interact with others.

☐ Activities engage students in higher-level thinking skills, including critical and creative thinking, analysis, and problem solving.

☐ Activities encourage active interactions that involve course content and personal communication.

☐ Resources and activities support learning outcomes.

☐ An online space (e.g. discussion board, social network) is in place for students to meet outside the class.

☐ There are sufficient opportunities for learners to work collaboratively.

☐ Learners are encouraged to interact with others (fellow classmates, course guests, etc.) and benefit from their experience and expertise.

☐ Procedures for group activities are specified so that students are aware of their role and responsibility in collaborative activities.

Chapter 7

Resources that Engage

Context—What lies in the periphery of simplicity is definitely not peripheral...

How directed can   How directionless can
I stand to feel?   ←——————→   I afford to be?

Source: Maeda (2006), 6th law of simplicity

Now that you understand how a small collection of activities work online (see Chapter 6), you can enhance them with some of the resources covered in this chapter. The students will be able to do the same.

Resources break the monotony of solid text and add dimension to the learning experience. Provide students with a media-rich resource list or guidance for finding their own resources. This encourages students to go beyond the required materials and investigate on their own.

Online resources covered in this chapter include:

- **Text-based supplemental resources**—real-world examples accessible from online sources.

- **Images**—photos, screenshots, charts, graphs, illustrations, etc.

- **Audio and video** recordings.

- **Voices and perspectives** from the class.

- **Expert voices**—practitioners and academics.

- **Experiences** from the field.

- Free web-based **tools and resources**.

Note

If you are adept at using the internet to access and use resources, you may just need to flip through this section. The basics are here for those of you who are not so experienced.

The online learning experience is enhanced by the use of textual examples, images, multimedia, and web-based applications. You can:

- illuminate the topic;

- add variety;

- enable the introduction of other viewpoints to encourage critical thinking;

- connect with others in the real world;

- provide concrete examples; and

- address different learning styles.

This chapter is supplemented by instructions on the website, on how to find and create resources.

7.1   Text-based Supplemental Resources

In many fields, texts are the core category for online supplemental resources. Well-chosen real-world text resources support and enrich teacher-made and textbook content. In a classroom setting, such resources have generally been delivered to students in the form of handouts and reserve reference materials. Ideally, they are accessible in an authentic format.

Here are some examples of text-based resources:

- quotes, literary reviews, and critiques

- newspapers and magazines

Reprinted with permission

- historical speeches and documents

- business documents, plans, letters, statistics, reports, and case studies

International Education
CONИECT

| About Us | Our Sites | Our Partners | Contact Us |

Reprinted with permission

- scientific studies, documents, and experiments

- math problems, arguments, and examples, and

- international, political, and cultural documents and information.

Many text-based materials are accessible through institutional online library services or the internet. If something is assigned or recommended to students to retrieve, be sure they can all get to it. Provide direct links. Before the course is set to begin, check that all links are working. Also, check that the materials are up-to-date.

 Resource material is accessible to all students in commonly used formats.

Encourage students to find and contribute resources that enhance the topic. In some cases, they will find examples that the teacher was not aware of. This promotes a learner-centered class. Both the students and the teacher learn in such a situation.

Note: It is important to follow copyright law. Many resources on the internet are available free for educational purposes. We will provide you with some very good copyright-free sources in this guide. If you do not see any information on whether the resources are free when you first enter a site, look for information under "terms of use" or a similar head in one of the site's menus (at the top or bottom of the page).

The consequences of plagiarism, cheating, and failure to properly cite copyrighted material are emphasized.

For guidance on how to find what you are looking for, many university and public libraries offer helpful orientation sessions, either live or online. Alternatively, just keep honing your basic online search skills.

 For guidance on how to capture and embed text examples, refer to the website.

7.2   Images—Photos, Screenshots, Charts, Graphs, and Illustrations

Embedding images, when appropriate and supportive of learning, is a first and fairly simple step in enhancing your online course. Some fields, such as art, science, and medicine, cannot really be taught without images. This is true whether they are onsite or online. In others, such as literature, philosophy, and law, you may tend to use text exclusively. However, as we've said, teaching online requires special strategies to vary the presentation of materials.

☑ Courses include a variety of relevant multimedia to support learning (e.g. audio, video, recommended podcasts, illustrations, photographs, charts, and graphs).

Refer to the typical LMS editing toolbar in Figure 7.1 to see the icons that you click on to enable you to embed links, images, and audio/video in your course. The common image formats accepted by most LMSs are JPEG, GIF, and PNG. Make sure your images are saved in one of these formats.

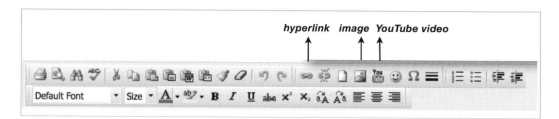

Figure 7.1 LMS toolbar

Epsilen

Reflection

Flip through this book. Use it as a model.

This guide has many images, charts, and screenshots to help you work through the content. More, including audio and video segments, are available on the website.

What if this guide were written without this rich array of images and resources? How would this affect your understanding of the subject? Could we have communicated issues of online course design as effectively?

If so, how? If not, why not?

What Kinds of Images Do You Need?

Scott Thornbury, a featured teacher (see page 175), created a linguistics course, *Language Analysis for Teachers*. Linguistics is certainly a text-based subject. In fact, most of his lessons are text-based. Scott constantly varies the activities in his presentations to engage the students. Yet, you will see, when looking at Scott's sample lesson (see page 173), that he uses images when helpful. He does this throughout the course when appropriate. None of the images are used gratuitously.

Scott has rethought the way he presents linguistics for an online environment. In the process, he enhances the subject matter and creates a learning environment that addresses a variety of learning styles.

When working with text-heavy subject matter, try to imagine how images might enhance your online presentation. With literature, for example, the visual arts, music, or fashion of the period may help students to understand the content and style of what they are studying.

Where do you find images to use in your online course? For those of you who know what kind of images you are looking for, explore the many sites that are sure to be there in your field. There are many different search engines available that

Figure 7.2 An "everything" search in Google

have different ways to search. Looking for images? In Google, you can do an "everything" search (see Figure 7.2). There you can find a selection of resources on your topic and the websites where they appear.

When the search results come up, Google gives you several options to refine the output, including images. See Figure 7.3 for an example of a refined image search.

Figure 7.3 The "images" result set from Google

Tip

Try using another search engine, such as Bing or Yahoo, from time to time. You will notice that the search results can be very different. Use the one that suits you best.

Those of you who are not sure of what kind of images to use can search for inspiration and ideas. First, look at what others have done. How have people who deal with the same topics added dimension by using images on their websites?

Once you have some general ideas of what might work for you, move to the second stage and look for specific images for your topic. These can be photos, illustrations, charts, graphs, diagrams, or screenshots. All are searchable through Google Images.

For teachers who find they are teaching the same courses repeatedly, searching for and adding resources can lead to fresh perspectives. This can be a refreshing and perhaps even inspiring activity for teachers.

For quantitative topics, create graphs and charts, when possible, to represent numerical information (see Figure 7.4). Pie charts, bar graphs, and line graphs are great ways to convey quantitative information to visual learners. It's critical that details such as the legend, axes, and labels of graphs and charts are readable, understandable, and clear.

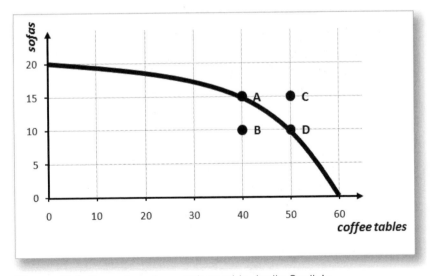

Figure 7.4 Examples of a graph used in Joelle Scally's Macroeconomics online course

A funny thing	happened	on the way to the forum
NP	VP	PP
Subject (= the actor or agent)	Verb (= a process or state)	Adverbial (= circumstantial information, such as time, place or manner)

Figure 7.5 A chart created by Scott Thornbury to illustrate sentence elements

Charts can also be a useful way to clarify concepts and organize information (see Figure 7.5).

☑ Details in images, graphs, charts, and diagrams are easy to see.

☑ Labeling in all presentation materials is accurate, readable, and clear.

7.3 Audio and Video

Audio and video address specific learning styles. They can also add a personal feel, real-world experiences, dynamic examples, and dimension to the learning module.

The internet is a good source of video material, and published videos are often available with textbooks. Making your own is another option.

Whether making audio and/or video clips is easy or even possible depends upon the equipment you have. Many computers come out-of-the box ready to make audio and video material, as do some mobile phones. If your computer is not set up, there are inexpensive, easy-to-use audio and video recorders on the market, such as the $100 Flip video recorder.

When linking to or embedding video or audio clips, it is important to provide students with a link to the media player, such as Flash, RealMedia, or QuickTime. However, video clips on YouTube do not require a player since YouTube is its own player.

 Refer to the website for the easiest way to find or make your own materials.

 The format of multimedia should be specified, with a direct link to a required plug-in when necessary.

7.4 Varying Voices and Perspectives

Resources, whether teacher- or student-made, pulled from the internet, or from guests to the class, give you the opportunity to bring other voices, opinions, and perspectives into the classroom. For example:

- Voices from the class—the teacher and students in various formats.

- Expert voices—practitioners and academics.

- Experiences from the field—workplace/worksite voices and situations.

The Teacher in Different Formats

One way to create textured presentation is by varying the way the teacher communicates with the class. When writing, for example, the teacher can alternate discussion board communications with blog postings and email as is appropriate. Embedded audio and video samples from the teacher provide relief from solidly textual communications.

Such variations enable students to experience the teacher from different perspectives. It also models how the students may present themselves.

Varying the way the teacher communicates can enhance content. Audio and video commentary can build in redundancy to clarify difficult concepts. It may be the source of anecdotal information, examples, and tips. The teacher may herself reflect on a topic she has asked the students to reflect on. Teachers can come up with good reasons to include such examples depending upon their style, priorities, and the content.

Keep audio and video segments short (2–5 minutes is a good size). This way, they read like a welcome break rather than another task. Watching long video clips can be tiresome. It's important to note that you are not replicating an onsite course lecture. Instead, you are creating a custom experience for the online student audience. Recording lectures from an onsite course tends to be dry because it was intended for an onsite audience to experience in a live format. The examples that follow show you how to design multimedia content appropriate for the online student audience.

Example 1: Narrated Support

In Figure 7.6, Scott Thornbury provides an audio explanation of a key concept in his linguistics course. Thinking of language in new ways requires some adjustment on the part of students. In this case, Scott is himself reflecting on a topic he has asked the students to reflect on. This also gives students another perspective on their teacher. You can see this audio in context on page 174.

☑ Audio and video material appearing within a lesson should be brief.

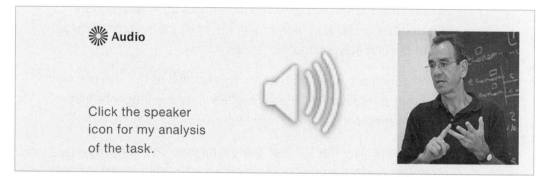

Figure 7.6 An audio recording in Scott Thornbury's online class
The New School/Matthew Sussman.

The Students in Different Formats

Once the teacher has included some audio and video clips into the course, she can suggest that the students do the same in their presentations. Share the tools you learn about at the end of this chapter with the students as is appropriate. However, it is important to emphasize again that **the length of audio and video segments should be relatively brief**.

Expert Voices—Practitioners and Academics

Example 1: Direct Expert Interaction

A guest speaker, whether a practitioner or an academic, brings another voice and a source of expertise into the online class. In a direct interaction, the guest speaker communicates directly with the students in some way. The guest should first be introduced to the students. Here are some examples:

- A reading assignment related to the guest.

- A summary biography and/or an example of the guest's work.

- A research assignment on some aspect of the guest's work, company, or institution.

- An audio or video clip of the guest in performance or being interviewed.

- An audio clip, slideshow, or video clip of a series of the guest's works.

How the guest is presented to the students will depend upon the nature of the guest's work and how this relates to what is being studied.

Next, the guest interacts with the students. Some examples:

- The teacher creates a discussion forum for the class to interact with one another over a few days or a week. The guest visits over this period of time and responds to students' posts.

- The guest visits a project website (wiki) and then comments or critiques it via audio, video, or in group discussion forums.

☑ **Learners are encouraged to interact with others (fellow classmates, course guests, etc.) and benefit from their experience and expertise.**

Example 2: Indirect Expert Interaction

In an indirect expert interaction, the students respond to the expert in some way, and the teacher comments and communicates with the students.

Figure 7.7 is an example that provides the students with another form of real-life input into the course. The students respond to the guest's blog posts and the teacher provides feedback on the students' posts.

This example is from Professor Lehrer's course on Advanced Business Writing taught at NYU. Note: The activity was modified for the purposes of this book.

Activity: PowerPoint Blog

Hi All: We have a guest writer for this week's blog—*Lucy Rivers*. She has written a blog about PowerPoint (yes, that is the correct spelling). Special thanks go to her for her effort. The blog has been posted in our online course, and can be found by clicking on **blogs**.

Please respond to her thoughts with your own by next Monday, February 8th. Make sure to use an outline to organize your thoughts, and compose your response **off line** so that you can proof it properly.

If you have any questions, please post them in the **Q&A discussion forum**.

Thanks

Professor Lehrer

Figure 7.7 An activity that brings in expert commentary

Example 3: Expert Audio and Video Clips (from the Internet)

It is fairly easy to find online mini-lectures that are freely available on the internet in all subject areas. At the writing of this book, one very prominent example is The Khan Academy (see Figure 7.8).

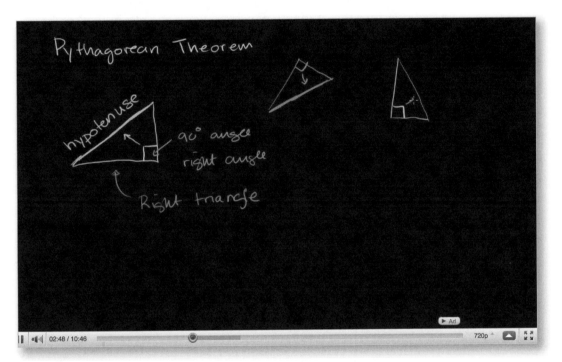

Figure 7.8 Khan Academy – Introduction to the Pythagorean theorem presentation
Reprinted with permission

> The goal of the Khan Academy is to use technology to provide a free, world-class education to anyone, anywhere. It is currently a library of 1176 videos... covering everything from basic arithmetic to advanced calculus, chemistry, economics and biology.
>
> www.khanacademy.org

The narrator explains the concepts while speaking and writing on the digital blackboard that is recorded as a video.

7.5	## Experiences from the Field

In practical study areas such as medicine, social work, and business, "field" refers to the term "field work." Resources from the field provide real life exposure to users, clients, patients, students, customers, and situations related to the class's area of study. The subjects are the kinds of people or situations that the students would be working with in the field they are studying.

For academic subjects such as languages, literature, and research, "field" refers to the subject area. Guests may include researchers, graduate students, writers, etc.

Field voices serve as a means to brings the voices and perspectives of different players into the class. Their perspectives may be cultural, educational, economic, social, or political. Be sure that the materials represent current issues.

This is an excellent way to expose students to the realities they will face and give them a real feel for the subject matter in a chosen field, occupation, or profession. Even if the field does not represent their primary area of study, such exposure enriches the learning experience.

In a practical field, this may also be a way to bring in current issues related to best practices. These could vary from discussions of how to do research, teach, create something, or set up a good interview, to the tone and content of doctor/patient, or teacher/student, or customer services manager/representative exchanges.

Example: Input from the Field

In another part of his course, Scott Thornbury makes audio recordings of a variety of players in the language teaching and learning field. Each comment is very short and to the point (see Figure 7.9).

✳ **Audio**

How important is language knowledge?

Listen to these five people responding to that question. Which of them best represents your own position?

Click on speaker to hear video.

The first two are **experienced teachers**;

1   2

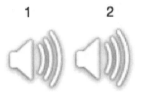

the third is a **relatively inexperienced teacher**;

3

the fourth is an advanced, Spanish-speaking, **student of English**;

4

and the fifth is a **teacher trainer**.

5

Figure 7.9

Teacher, peer-to-peer, guest, and automated feedback clarifies, amplifies, and extends the topic.

☑ Topics and materials are up-to-date and relevant.

☑ Materials are authentic or relate to real-life applications.

 Review and pick out some good examples of videos to show the class or ask students to review videos and post their favorite, with an explanation as to why they have chosen it. Set clear criteria for them to reinforce their choices and focus their search. This type of activity engages the student and can be time-saving for the teacher.

☑ Presentations of new knowledge and skills, activities, and assessments address a variety of learning styles.

7.6 Free Web-based Tools and Resources

 Web-based tools are programs that can help. The teacher is in the best position to determine what would add value to their content. On the website we introduce a series of tools with short descriptions and links. In most cases, we will provide tutorials and/or details on how to use the tool.

7.7 Accessibility

We end this chapter with last and very important point. Careful attention must be paid to ease of accessibility of resources. We emphasize especially these three points:

- **Format**—Whatever the resources, they must be made available to students in a format that they can access. For example, if you know that class videos will be in a Quicktime format, students should be informed early on in the course that they will need to have a Quicktime player installed. In addition a link to Quicktime downloads should always be within reach.

- **Links**—Cross-referencing is another area of accessibility that is critical. If a resource is not right there where it is referred to it should be available by clicking on a link. The clickable link itself should describe what it is linking to rather than be a URL, e.g. <u>Bing</u> rather than <u>www.bing.com</u>.

- **Portability**—Large files, videos, and audios should be available in some kind of portable format so that students can access and review them on the go. Text files should be downloadable as PDFs. Audios and videos should be downloadable so that they can be accessed on smartphones, iPads, iPods, or other such gadgets.

☑ Cross-referencing and links to items in other parts of the course are provided.

☑ When possible, course material is portable (e.g. text can be downloaded or printed out, material is transferable to other devices, and presentations can be downloaded, printed out, or saved).

Finally, this standard speaks for itself:

☑ Bibliographies and reference lists include a variety of resources, including web links, books, journals, video, and downloadable text and audio files as is appropriate.

7.8 Summary and Standards

This chapter has provided you with ways to include supplemental text, images, audio and video recordings, and web-based tools into your online course. Refer to Chapters 6 and 10 when thinking about incorporating resources for online presentations and activities.

☐ Resource material is accessible to all students in commonly used formats.

☐ Courses include a variety of relevant multimedia to support learning (e.g. audio, video, recommended podcasts, illustrations, photographs, charts, and graphs).

☐ The consequences of plagiarism, cheating, and failure to properly cite copyrighted material are emphasized.

- [ ] Details in images, graphs, charts, and diagrams are easy to see.

- [ ] Labeling in all presentation materials is accurate, readable, and clear.

- [ ] The format of multimedia should be specified, with a direct link to a required plug-in when necessary.

- [ ] Audio and video material appearing within a lesson should be brief.

- [ ] Learners are encouraged to interact with others (fellow classmates, course guests, etc.) and benefit from their experience and expertise.

- [ ] Teacher, peer-to-peer, guest, and automated feedback clarifies, amplifies, and extends the topic.

- [ ] Topics and materials are up-to-date and relevant.

- [ ] Materials are authentic or relate to real-life applications.

- [ ] Presentations of new knowledge and skills, activities, and assessments address a variety of learning styles.

- [ ] Cross-referencing and links to items in other parts of the course are provided.

- [ ] When possible, course material is portable (e.g. text can be downloaded or printed out, material is transferable to other devices, and presentations can be downloaded, printed out, or saved).

- [ ] Direct links are provided to course materials and resources.

- [ ] Links are working and correct.

- [ ] Bibliographies and reference lists include a variety of resources, including web links, books, journals, video, and downloadable text and audio files as is appropriate.

Chapter 8   Assessment and Feedback

This chapter covers the important elements of assessment and feedback, with specific considerations for online teaching. Key elements covered are:

- Assessment is tied directly to learning outcomes.

- Assessment is varied and ongoing.

- Teacher feedback is timely.

- Peer-to-peer feedback is encouraged.

- Learner expectations and requirements are clear.

- Grading criteria is evident.

8.1   Assessing Learning Outcomes

Keep in mind that assessment processes are clearly and directly tied to the learning outcomes of the course. Performance is measured through the products of the learner's work. Products may include papers, assignments, tests, quizzes, digital presentations, and projects. Class participation interactions with peers, teachers, and course guests are also indicators of learner performance.

Refer to page 165. This is the introduction to the first week of Kristen Sosulski's *Collaboration Technologies* online course at NYU. It includes specific outcomes for a week online. Note that the wording is clear and definite. The terms **identify**, **describe**, **apply**, and **categorize** are **measurable** and relate to a range of thinking skills.

Refer to page 168 for an example of a **class participation activity** from Kristen's course that is designed to measure student achievement of the learning outcomes. This is a two-part activity. This example demonstrates the relationship between learning outcomes (what is being assessed) and how those outcomes are being assessed. Note the specifics on grading, due dates and times, and location within the LMS where the students should go to complete the assignment.

☑ **The relationship between learning outcomes and assessments is evident.**

☑ **Assessments determine the degree to which the learners have achieved the required learning outcomes.**

☑ **The size of and due date for graded assignments are reasonable.**

8.2 Ongoing and Varied Assessment

> Rather than using just one method, robust assessment requires the critical analysis of multiple forms of evidence that learning outcomes have been attained.
>
> Reeves (2006: 304)

Assess online students on an ongoing basis. This gives them multiple opportunities to improve upon and reinforce their knowledge and skills. Assessing online learners regularly highlights where the students are in their learning process.

Ongoing assessment provides:

- quantifiable evidence of learner engagement and participation;

- opportunities to give feedback to learners;

- demonstrable measures of learner progress within the course; and

- an opportunity for learners to test and apply their knowledge and skills.

It is also important to evaluate learner performance based on a variety of assessment types, (i.e. not just tests). **Not all skills and knowledge can be evaluated with the same measurement technique.** Varied types of activities are encouraged and are easy to design for online once you know the basics. These can include online class discussions and group projects. This also builds in a safeguard against cheating. When you have multiple assessments in different forms, you can better gauge the student's performance.

 Course includes ongoing and frequent assessment.

 Graded assignments are varied (e.g. special projects, reflective assignments, research papers, case studies, presentations, group work, etc.).

8.3 Teacher Feedback

Good teacher feedback on assessments promotes and improves online learning. Specifically, the role of feedback is to:

- expand upon the learner's knowledge;

- help the learner understand how to improve and progress within the course; and

- clarify misconceptions and misunderstandings, and correct mistakes.

Ongoing assessment engages the learner throughout the course. This is especially true when teacher feedback is timely. Regular and timely feedback helps students to improve. It should highlight areas that need improvement, present suggestions for future learning, and indicate where progress has been made.

It is important that you communicate when and how students will receive feedback on their work. In an onsite course, the teacher may do this through a class announcement. In an online class, the teacher can **use the announcements tool to communicate to learners when and how feedback is given on a particular assignment. Refer back to Chapter 3 to review writing announcements.**

 Teacher feedback is provided in a timely fashion.

8.4 Other Types of Feedback

As previously discussed, feedback from the teacher should be continual, with regular opportunities for assessment of the learner's work. In addition, feedback can come from peers and class guests who have expertise in the course's content. Refer to the Assessment and Feedback Plan in Figure 8.1 to see how other types of feedback are provided to learners in an online course. The plan clearly indicates who is to give feedback and when.

Peer-to-peer Feedback

When learners receive feedback on their work from their peers, it achieves the following:

- Learners feel that the products of their work are not only relevant to the teacher, but that a larger audience is evaluating and commenting on their work.

- Learners learn how to critically assess the work of others.

- Assessing the work of others may lead to self-reflection in approaching their own work.

- Multiple perspectives on the same topic may lead to richer understandings and synthesis.

When requiring students to provide feedback to others on their work, set up the criteria for evaluation. This is critical for group projects, where each member evaluates one another's contributions.

Guest Feedback

Feedback from guests, such as experts in the field, can tie the activity to a real-world context for the learner. In an online course, it is easy to involve guests from anywhere in the world. Check with your institution to see how to include guests in your online course.

Automatic Computer-Generated Feedback

Most LMSs are equipped with a testing tool that enables teachers to design online test with instantaneous feedback. Feedback that is generated automatically should be descriptive. Explanations accompany each answer and describe why the learner's selection was correct or incorrect. Keep in mind that automatic feedback is especially good for periodic self-assessments. Use teacher, peer-to-peer, guest, and automated feedback to clarify, amplify, and extend a topic.

☑ Teacher, peer-to-peer, guest, and automated feedback clarifies, amplifies, and extends the topic.

☑ Criteria and procedures for peer review and evaluation are clear.

☑ Self-correcting and self-assessment activities are used throughout the course to enable learners to vary the pace of their learning as is appropriate to the subject matter.

Table 8.1 presents a partial Assessment and Feedback Plan for a 6-week course. This is a tool that teachers can use to assist in their planning about when and how feedback is given. Each activity type is mapped to a given week within the course and a corresponding grade percentage. Notice the number of automated (i.e. computer-corrected) practice exercises. Note: The feedback is immediate. This is one of the benefits of an online course.

W **The full chart and a template are available on the website.**

With this Assessment and Feedback Plan, the learner is engaged throughout a 6-week course. Specifically, there are three visible points of engagement for each week of the course. In this example, there are un-graded activities (Practice Exercises) and graded activities (Class Discussions, Online Journaling Activity, and a Group Project). **Teacher and peer-to-peer feedback is regular.** In addition, the Group Project presents an opportunity for feedback from the teacher, peers, and a class guest.

Table 8.1 An Assessment and Feedback Plan for the first two weeks of an online course

Assessment and Feedback Plan

Week #	Learner Activities	% of Grade	Feedback Given By	Feedback Turnaround
1	Practice Exercise	0%	Automated	Immediately
	Class Discussion	5%	Teacher Peers	Throughout the week's discussion
	Online Journal	5%	Teacher	Within a week
2	Practice Exercise	0%	Automated	Immediately
	Class Discussion	5%	Teacher Peers	Throughout the week's discussion
	Group Project	10%	Teacher Peers Guest	Within a week

Drafting an Assessment and Feedback Plan is an essential tool for the teacher of an online course. It serves as a reminder of when grading and feedback are required. It also outlines the stages of learner and teacher engagement throughout the duration of the course. To begin designing your plan, refer to Figure 8.1 below and use the online template. Think about the following:

- What are the key assignments, quizzes, and activities?

- Which activities are graded and which ones are not?

- Who will be giving feedback and when?

☑ Students know when and how they will receive feedback from instructors.

☑ Graded elements are clearly distinguished from those that are ungraded.

☑ The relationship between graded elements and the final grade is clear.

8.5 Setting Learner Expectations

- Clear grading criteria clarify learner expectations for each assessment.

- Each graded item is explained clearly in the syllabus accompanied by a percentage designation.

- Grading criteria are outlined in the course syllabus and corresponding assignments or activities.

- The grading criteria detail how each item's score correlates to the specific requirements for each assignment or activity (this can be done using a rubric).

- For un-graded items, it is still important to specify expectations in order to make learners aware of the criteria for excellent performance and/or work.

- The graded items are recorded in the online grade book.

Note
This approach is not uniform across all LMSs.

The online grade book allows the learners to track their progress within the course and check immediately when a grade has been assigned. See Figure 8.1 for a view of a single student's progress as noted in the online grade book.

Assignment	Points		Percentage	Grade
Participation 1 5.00% of Final Grade View Rubric	4.75	/ 5.00	95.00	A
Participation 2 5.00% of Final Grade View Rubric	5.00	/ 5.00	100.00	A
Participation 3 5.00% of Final Grade View Rubric	5.00	/ 5.00	100.00	A
Participation 4 5.00% of Final Grade View Rubric	5.00	/ 5.00	100.00	A
Participation 5 5.00% of Final Grade View Rubric	3.00	/ 5.00	60.00	C+
Project 1 20.00% of Final Grade	94.00	/ 100.00	94.00	A

Figure 8.1
A view of a single student's progress in the online grade book from the teacher's perspective

The following items must be communicated to the learner for each online assignment and activity:

- activity title
- instructions and requirements
- grading criteria
- due date
- location for submission (discussion forum, drop box, blog), and
- where and when the learner will receive teacher feedback.

☑ Grading criteria are outlined in the course syllabus and within the assignment or activity itself.

☑ Students are given clear expectations and criteria for assignments. Examples are included for clarification when needed.

☑ Students can easily track their progress.

8.6 Assessment of Activities

Table 8.2 presents the general **productive** and **reflective** activity types covered in Chapter 6 and corresponding assessment strategies. Examples of assessment measurements are provided for class participation and peer-to-peer evaluation of group projects.

Class Discussion and Class Participation

Class participation in an online course is a critical support for online engagement. Assessing learner engagement throughout the online course motivates and guides the learner.

Learners must actively contribute to class discussions. This requires posting regularly to the forum, at least two or three times per week. Setting up small weekly class participation activities supports active participation.

Classroom participation in an online course typically takes place in the **discussion forum**. These online discussions

Table 8.2 General assessments for different activity types

Activity	Assessment Strategy
Class Discussions and Class Participation	A class participation **rubric** is completed by students as a check to ensure they have fulfilled the criteria. Student participation is evaluated by the teacher using the rubric and the specific activity requirements.
Online Journaling	Student self-assessment and informal teacher feedback.
Shared Knowledge Base	Teacher assesses the contributions of each individual and/or group.
Practice Exercises (sometimes self-assessment)	Teacher assesses exercises for participation, rather than for correctness or incorrectness. Student assesses his or her own progress based on teacher or automatic computer-generated feedback.
Group Projects	Teacher assesses the group project as a whole. Team members complete a peer assessment. Teacher reviews peer assessment and factors in the student's individual grade for the group project.

should account for between 15 percent and 30 percent of the course grade. Active participation in discussions cultivates community within a course. It also provides the teacher with a clear indication of each learner's level of engagement.

In the **syllabus**, specify the course expectations for participation. To foster participation, the requirements are clearly outlined and class participation counts toward the final grade. The rubric in Table 8.3 illustrates how the grading for class participation can be defined. **A rubric is a tool that "defines the performance levels for each gradable activity element"** (Conrad & Donaldson, 2004: 26). The rubric in Table 8.3 describes the level of performance expected for levels of quality, accuracy, and timeliness. Specifically, "rubrics help the student figure out how their project[s], [assignments, activities, and participation] will be evaluated" (ALTEC, 2008: paragraph 1).

Teacher feedback is provided to students through comments in the discussion forum. The teacher also provides a grade for each activity in the grade book (see Figure 8.3). Most LMSs have a grade book. This is another form of feedback for those graded activities. In this example, each class participation activity is worth 5 percent of the grade. Each activity is assessed based on three criteria (quality, accuracy, and timeliness) on a 0 to 5 point scale.

This concrete approach clarifies the relationship between class participation and the course grade. It also advises learners that participation is assessed throughout the course.

Reflection

Think about how you plan to assess class participation.

If you require the students to participate in an online asynchronous discussion for a specified time period, you need to state this clearly.

Consider the following questions:

- How many posts per week will be required?

- How will the quality of each post be measured?

- Will the time between posts be important?

Table 8.3 An example of a class participation rubric (from Kristen Sosulski's course) used to assess student postings in the discussion forum

Evaluation Criteria	Does Not Meet Any of the Requirements	Partially Meets Requirements	Mostly Meets Requirements	Meets All Requirements	Exceeds Requirements
Quality	Contributions to the online class discussion are well written, proofread, and directly relevant to the discussion topic.				
	0	1–2	3	4	5
Accuracy	All contributions are supported with evidence, if required. Sharing personal experiences is essential to this course, however, applying and referencing the salient course readings, cases, and other literature is critical.				
	0	1–2	3	4	5
Timeliness	Contributions are made within the assigned time period.				
	0	1–2	3	4	5

Assignment		Max Points		Percentage of Grade		Rubric
Participation 1	*	05	*	5.00	%	Class Participation Rubric
Participation 2	*	05	*	5.00	%	Class Participation Rubric
Participation 3	*	05	*	5.00	%	Class Participation Rubric
Participation 4	*	05	*	5.00	%	Class Participation Rubric
Participation 5	*	05	*	5.00	%	Class Participation Rubric

Figure 8.2 An example of class participation grades as noted in the online grade book within the LMS

Reprinted with permission

 Class participation/discussion should account for 15–30 percent of the final grade.

 Criteria/rubrics clearly inform learners as to how they will be assessed on specific assignments, such as online class participation.

Group Projects

Group projects require teacher and peer-to-peer assessment. The best-designed team projects include **team and individual assessment** by the teacher (Educause, 2010) in addition to **peer-to-peer assessment**.

The assessment of **individual student performance** in a group project can be tricky. Be sure to delineate or have the team assign roles to each member. The roles and responsibilities of each student in the team should be clear.

Personal Perspective

Kristen Sosulski

I take a democratic approach to teamwork. In my online courses, when I assign a group project, I require that the team identify a project manager/leader who will take minutes on all the group meetings that include roles, responsibilities, key action items, and next steps with due dates. This helps me assess the work of individuals within a team. I then review the peer-to-peer assessments of each team member by the team. This gives me a clear understanding of who did what.

The teacher can structure the peer-to-peer assessment by providing a peer assessment form (see Table 8.4). The peer assessment form measures the participation of all team members. Students rate each team member according to a prescribed set of criteria. These forms can be designed for students to complete at the end of a group project, or periodically throughout the project work.

Tip

Some LMSs come equipped with survey tools to help you develop these peer assessment forms. An alternative is to use free online tools such as Survey Monkey or Google Forms to create an online peer evaluation form, and send the link to the students. You can then view the results online. You can also include an option for students to either put their name on the form or keep it anonymous.

 Another example of a peer assessment form can be found on the website. It provides a way for each member of the group to assign a grade percentage for each team member. The grades for all team members must equal 100 percent.

 For teacher assessment and feedback on team projects considering developing a group project assessment rubric, see the website.

Self-assessment

Incorporating self-assessment and reflective activities helps students recognize where they are in their own learning and how they can vary their pace (Quality Matters, 2006). This aids in learners' understanding of what they know and don't know.

Non-pressured low-risk forms of feedback, such as computer-generated feedback, enable learners to test their knowledge privately. Avoid specifically grading all assignments and activities. Instead, you may credit students in projects and work where the results of their reflective work have made a difference. Un-graded assessments can reduce the stress on the learners and encourage a reflective process.

Table 8.4 A simple peer assessment form for assessing member participation in group projects

Group Project Peer Evaluation Form						
Project # 2—Group A						
Criteria		No participation in group meetings or deliverables.	Minimal participation in group meetings. Contributions to group deliverables were incomplete or incorrect.	Participated in most or all group meetings. Marginal contributions to deliverables, but contributions were of value to the group.	Participated in all group meetings. Completed the assigned deliverables based on his/her role. Contributions were of value to the group.	Participated in all group meetings. Went beyond the assigned deliverables. Regularly volunteered for additional roles and tasks.
Members	Role in Project					
Kelly Brown	Project Manager					
James Dixon	Researcher					
Yelena Jones	Writer					
Joseph Zu	Presenter					

☑ Self-correcting and self-assessment activities are used throughout the course to enable learners to vary the pace of their learning as is appropriate to the subject matter.

Figure 8.3 is a self-assessment from Scott Thornbury's class. Notice that it comes at the very beginning of the lesson. This gives students a sense of how much they already know about the topic. When they finish with the test, they can click on an answer link and self-assess.

Introduction to vowel sounds

Learning Outcome
By the end of this section you should be able to explain how vowel sounds contribute to intelligibility.

Task 4.1.1

Test yourself: how much do you remember about phonology so far?

1. The study of speech sounds and sound production in general is called _____.
2. The smallest element of sound in a language which is recognized by a native speaker as making a difference in meaning is called a _____.
3. The study of how speech sounds are produced, used, and distinguished in a specific language is called _____.
4. A vocal sound made without audible stopping of breath is a _____.
5. Sounds that are made when the airflow from the lungs is obstructed in some way are called _____.
6. The ridge immediately behind the top teeth is called the _____ ridge.
7. Voiced sounds are those where the _____ are made to vibrate.
8. A consonant sound that is produced by the build-up and sudden release of air is called a _____.
9. A consonant sound that is formed by obstructing the airflow at the two lips is called a _____.
10. The sound /f/ is to /v/ as /k/ is to _____?
11. Write the sentence Is this Jeb's sixth fish in phonemic script.
12. What English word begins and ends with the sound /t ʃ/?

View Answers —————————————➤

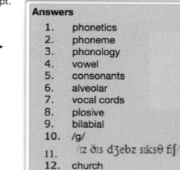

Answers
1. phonetics
2. phoneme
3. phonology
4. vowel
5. consonants
6. alveolar
7. vocal cords
8. plosive
9. bilabial
10. /g/
11. /ɪz ðɪs dʒebz sɪksθ fɪʃ/
12. church

Figure 8.3 An example of a practice exercise with pop-up answers used for students to self-assess

8.7   What About Exams and Testing?

Exams and testing are common ways to assess student knowledge retention. They are appropriate ways to assess your students depending upon the subject area and/or how they are devised. A combination of multiple-choice testing and essays can provide the instructor with a sense of the students' understanding and the ways in which they can apply their knowledge to explain, critique, assess, and discuss the course content. The idea is to provide frequent and varied assessments to ensure students are learning, and provide low-risk assessment opportunities for students.

8.8   Summary and Standards

The standards set forth below have been discussed throughout this chapter. Use these standards to inform the design of your assessments for your online course.

Assessment

☐ The relationship between learning outcomes and assessments is evident.

☐ Assessments determine the degree to which the learners have achieved the required learning outcomes.

☐ Course includes ongoing and frequent assessment.

☐ Self-correcting and self-assessment activities are used throughout the course to enable learners to vary the pace of their learning as is appropriate to the subject matter.

☐ Class participation/discussion should account for 15–30 percent of the final grade.

Evaluation and Grading

☐ The size of and due date for graded assignments are reasonable.

☐ Graded assignments are varied (e.g. special projects, reflective assignments, research papers, case studies, presentations, group work, etc.).

☐ Criteria and procedures for peer review and evaluation are clear.

☐ Graded elements are clearly distinguished from those that are ungraded.

☐ The relationship between graded elements and the final grade is clear.

☐ Grading criteria are outlined in the course syllabus and within the assignment or activity itself.

☐ Students are given clear expectations and criteria for assignments. Examples are included for clarification when needed.

☐ Students can easily track their progress.

☐ Criteria/rubrics clearly inform learners as to how they will be assessed on specific assignments, such as online class participation.

Feedback

☐ Teacher, peer-to-peer, guest, and automated feedback clarifies, amplifies, and extends the topic.

☐ Teacher feedback is provided in a timely fashion.

☐ Students know when and how they will receive feedback from instructors.

Chapter 9

Building the Course Foundation: Outcomes, Syllabus, and Course Outline

This is it. This is the part of the guide that walks you through the process of building your course. You will notice that this section is relatively lean and straightforward.

Up to this point in the book, we have been laying out the substance. The knowledge, skills, and standards groundwork have been covered. We have looked closely at what makes up a lesson. Here we will work on creating the foundation and, in Chapter 10, creating the body of the course. The basic elements covered are:

- learning outcomes
- the online syllabus
- the course outline
- from course outline to lessons.

9.1 The Critical Importance of Learning Outcomes

Learning outcomes are at the core of a process that creates courses and programs that follow through on their promises. As such, there are learning outcomes expressed at every stage in the process.

Open—Openness simplifies complexity.
Maeda (2006), 2nd law of simplicity

We have already referred to the importance of using learning outcomes as an assurance or guarantee to learners that the online course will be as comprehensive and rigorous as its onsite equivalent. The learning outcomes for both should be identical.

They also provide the teacher with clear guidelines for developing an online course. We are therefore providing a fairly comprehensive review of what the learning outcomes are and how to write them.

Because a good number of you may already be using learning outcomes, we will not cover them in detail within this chapter. Instead, refer to Appendix A, where we provide rationales for using outcomes, the argument for using outcomes instead of objectives, and a guide for writing learning outcomes. We will, however, include all related standards here.

☑ Learning outcomes are measurable and specific.

☑ The wording used to define learning outcomes is clear and definite.

☑ Course material is sufficient and directly related to learning outcomes.

☑ Resources and activities support learning outcomes.

☑ Assessments determine the degree to which the learners have achieved the required learning outcomes.

9.2 The Online Syllabus

An online syllabus contains many of the same elements as an onsite syllabus. The basic categories include Course Title, Course Name, Course Description, Course Objectives, Evaluation Plan, Grading, Required Readings, Recommended Readings, and Course Outline. The syllabus contains a very detailed course outline, and a thorough explanation of how the online course is organized and will operate.

 For a full example of an online syllabus, see the website.

A detailed syllabus is the core organizing document for the teacher and the students. It is where students go to find out everything they need to know about the course requirements, evaluation process, contact information, schedule, and institutional policy.

Given the open flexibility of online study, it is especially important that the online syllabus be comprehensive and clear. It is the backbone of the online course. An ongoing Q&A discussion forum (see page 86) is a good place to clarify syllabus information.

The syllabus should be written to give students a clear sense of the teacher's expectations for performance. When a student finishes reading the syllabus, she should have a clear sense of what it will take to achieve the course learning outcomes and succeed.

For the teacher, it is also the framework for course development. Just as students have different learning styles, teachers have different organizational, planning, and teaching styles. Laying out the process of building up your course incrementally may work for some and not for others. However, the syllabus is the starting point no matter what your approach.

Special Characteristics of an Online Syllabus

We recommend that the online syllabus include additional items that are specific to online needs. These include:

- a communication strategy;

- a clear description of the course time frame and format;

- guidelines for online class participation;

- technical requirements and support; and

- a detailed course outline (with start and end dates).

Communication Strategy

A communication strategy is a description of how and when students can contact you via email, phone, chat, etc. It's important to indicate when you will return emails and phone messages (see Figure 9.1, page 148). Some people even recommend setting up an electronic communication policy (Watrall, 2010). Never underestimate how confusing and messy things can get without such a strategy.

Communication Strategy

There are several ways you can contact me:

- **Office Hours**. I am available for onsite office hours every Wednesday from 4:00 p.m. to 5:00 p.m. and online by appointment. Please call (xxx) xxx-xxxx to schedule an appointment.

- **Phone Appointment**. I am available for phone appointments. Please contact me to schedule an appointment.

- **Email**. I am available by email and will respond within 24 to 48 hours. For urgent matters, I would suggest following up by phone.

- **Question and Answer Discussion Forum**. Always check the Question and Answer discussion forum to ask a question of the class and see if a response has been posted to your question.

Figure 9.1 An example of Kristen Sosulski's communication strategy within her online course syllabus

Course Format and Time Frame

Format

This course is asynchronous. We will not meet in the classroom. All activities and assignments will be completed online using the LMS. You will participate when convenient within a fixed period of time (e.g. between June 1 and June 6, 11:59 p.m. EST)

Time Frame

- This is a **six-week** online course.

- Our online week begins on a Monday and ends on Sunday.

- The first day of the online course is Monday, June 28 and the last day is August 4.

Students are expected to follow the course outline and engage and participate in the activities outlined in each weekly **lesson**. Students are required to keep pace with class, follow the course outline, and complete necessary readings and assignments by the designated due date.

Due dates are expressed in day and hour EST (Eastern Standard Time). Students are responsible for adjusting due date to their time zone.

Figure 9.2 Course time frame and format within the online course syllabus

Course Time Frame and Format

The online course time frame is different than it is onsite. In the syllabus, clearly explain the format of the course (i.e. asynchronous) to the students. Explain that due dates and times are expressed with reference to a particular time zone (e.g. GMT, EST). Also, describe the start date and end date for the course, and how this corresponds to the beginning and ending of each module (see Figure 9.2).

Guidelines for Class Participation

Students should be required to contribute substantially to the discussion forum at a minimum of two to three times per week. Be sure to include the requirements for class participation in your syllabus and count those activities as part of the course grade (see Figure 9.3). A rubric that outlines the criteria for evaluating class participation leaves little room for confusion (see Chapter 8).

Course Requirements

Evaluation Criteria	Does Not Meet Any of the Requirements	Partially Meets Requirements	Mostly Meets Requirements	Meets All Requirements	Exceeds Requirements
Quality	Contributions to the online class discussion are well written, proofread, and directly relevant to the discussion topic.				
	0	1–2	3	4	5
Accuracy	All contributions are supported with evidence, if required. Sharing personal experiences is essential to this course, however applying and referencing the salient course readings, cases, and other literature is critical.				
	0	1–2	3	4	5
Timeliness	Contributions were made within the assigned time period.				
	0	1–2	3	4	5

Figure 9.3 Class participation rubric described in the course syllabus

Criteria/rubrics clearly inform learners as to how they will be assessed on specific assignments, such as online class participation.

Technical Requirements and Support

Do not forget to include how students can get help if they are having trouble accessing (logging in to) the online course. Also, refer students to the technical requirements of the LMS (see Figure 9.4).

 Contact information to advisors and technical help is provided in the syllabus.

Technical Requirements and Support

The online portion of this course will be held via NYU-SCPS Online. Help is available at:

- http://online.scps.nyu.edu

Your user name and password was emailed to your NYU email address five days prior to the course start. Please contact me immediately if you are unable to access the course website.

For an overview on how the course works go to:

- http://distancelearning.scps.nyu.edu/screencasts

Live Online Group Meetings

Your group may want to meet online in real time. For the live online meetings, test out your system to ensure your computer is configured properly at:

- http://snipurl.com/liveclassroom

Online Technical Support

If you need assistance contact the NYU SCPS HELP DESK

- North America: (877) 395-2996
- International: (216) 454-1153
- Email: scps.distancelearning.helpdesk@nyu.edu

Figure 9.4 Technical requirements within the online course syllabus

Course Outline

The online course outline is a calendar and a to do list, and presents a sequence of events, assignments, readings, activities, and course deliverables.

See Figure 9.5 for a partial online course outline from Kristen Sosulski's course. Notice how the course is organized in units and lessons. Each lesson represents 1 week in the online course.

 All graded activities are listed upfront in the syllabus.

 The manner of submission for graded assignments is clear.

The syllabus components box (pages 152–153) is a comprehensive checklist for the essential points that need to be covered in a syllabus and a course outline. Many items are just a carry-over from the onsite syllabus.

Course Outline

Lesson	Topic	Reading	Assignment
UNIT I: INTRODUCTION TO COLLABORATION FORMATS, TECHNOLOGIES, AND VIRTUAL TEAMS			
1. 06/28 –07/04	Introduction to Collaboration Technologies and Virtual Teamwork	Course Syllabus Kock, Chapters 1 & 3	**Activity 1** (Parts 1-3) Due 6/30
	Categories of eCollaborative technologies. Reflecting on your how you use them.		**Assignment 1** Part 1 Due 7/2 Part 2 Due 7/4
2. 07/05 – 07/11	Team dynamics, synchronous, and asynchronous technologies Online team meetings	16 Tips for Using Email More Effectively Meeting face to face or remotely: Evaluating the options Responsibility Chart Using asynchronous meetings to boost performance, accelerate results Davidson, p. 296-326 Davidson, p. 323-326	**Assignments 2a & 2b** Due 7/11
UNIT II: ORGANIZING FORMAL COLLABORATION			
3. 7/12 – 07/18	Collaborative Sensemaking and Group Development	Clark, Donald. Survey. Kock, Chapter 4	**Assignment 3a** Due 7/14 **Assignment 3b** Due 7/18 **Group Project 1** Due 7/18

Figure 9.5 A partial example of an online course outline

Syllabus Components

Basic Course Information

- Session (e.g. Fall, 2010)

- Course title and number/section

- Instructor name and email

- Academic credits

- Prerequisite(s)

Course Time Frame and Format

- Format (i.e. **asynchronous** or **blended**, with an explanation).

- Number of weeks online.

- First and last day of the online course. Note any holidays.

- Weekly start and end day for each lesson (e.g. the online week begins on Tuesday and ends on Monday).

- **Due date/time zone**: due dates are expressed in day, hour, and time zone (e.g. GMT, EST). Students are responsible for adjusting the due date to their time zone. The time zone expressed will most likely be that of the teacher (see Figure 9.2).

Course Description

A summary overview of the course.

Learning Outcomes

These express what the learner will know or be able to do at the end of the course.

Communication Strategy

Provides a space and place for the teacher to clearly outline their availability and response time within the online course (see Figure 9.1).

Department and Academic Advisement

This contact information connects the course with the academic program and/or department.

Technical Requirements

The contact information for online technical support and resources (see Figure 9.4).

Course Requirements

1. **Assignments**. The overview of assignments, such as number of papers, projects, participation in discussion forums, tests quizzes, group projects, readings, etc.

2. **Assessment and Feedback Plan**.
   See Table 8.1.

3. **Activity grade percentages**.
   List how grades will be determined and the weight of each type of activity in determining a final grade.

4. **Criteria for class participation**.
   Students should be required to contribute substantially to the discussion forum, a minimum of three times per week. A rubric that outlines the criteria for evaluating class participation leaves little room for confusion (see Chapter 9).

5. **Policy on due dates and lateness**.
   Establishes clear rules and penalties for late assignments.

6. The manner of submission for graded assignments is clear.

Link to Institutional Academic Policy

Statement on plagiarism and cheating, and honor code.

Course Outline

The online course outline is calendar, to-do list, and presents a sequence of events, assignments, readings, activities, and course deliverables.

See Figure 9.5 for an example of a course outline.

You may find that you want to use all of the items listed here and add some. Or you may want to leave things out. For example, if your course recommends reading time-sensitive materials, you will not be able to list them ahead of time. But you can explain where the readings will come from and how much you expect the students to read. All critical information for succeeding should be in the syllabus.

 A syllabus template is available on the website.

☑ A syllabus including contact information, an outline, requirements, and guidelines is accessible from the start of the course and throughout.

☑ Instructions and requirements are stated simply, clearly, and logically.

☑ Consequences of missed deadlines and insufficient class participation are clearly stated and fair.

☑ The consequences of plagiarism, cheating, and failure to properly cite copyrighted material are emphasized.

9.3 Using the Course Outline to Structure Your Online Course

You are now set up to plan your course week by week. As we've pointed out before, a good place to start is by considering these three areas:

1. Begin with the learning outcomes. Each unit will have at least one learning outcome. Let's say, for example, that a learning outcome states: "The students will be able to create an organized and effective promotional slideshow of a physical product (of some kind)." The lessons that make up the unit will have their own outcomes. The first in this case might be: "The student will be able to outline the qualities of an effective, promotional slide presentation on a given product."

2. Working backwards, you next plan out what assessments you will need to assure that the learning outcomes have been met. The main assessment for the unit will be the completed slideshow. The students will be graded on how well they do on the project. The smaller assessments for each module will build the students' skills so that they acquire the knowledge and skills they need to do the final project.

3. Next, using the assessments as the measure of your content, you lay out the knowledge, skills, and steps needed to enable the students to succeed at the final project—in this case, creating the professional slideshow. The first module might have them look at and analyze good and bad examples of related presentations. The challenge is to now set up the activities and resources to present the knowledge and skills to the students using effective pedagogical design. Do this unit by unit within the course, lesson by lesson within each unit, and, finally, step by step within each section.

At this point, you should have all the background knowledge you need to do this.

 Content elements are presented in a logical sequence.

 Pedagogical steps build progressively, one upon the other, as is appropriate to the subject matter.

9.4   Building the Lessons and Sections

Units and lessons are really just organizing structures. The meat of the course is within the sections/segments, or the chunks within each lesson.

A Course Walk Through

Let's look at Scott Thornbury's course on Language Analysis for Teachers (pages 156–160). First, look at the course description and learning outcomes in Figure 9.6.

Language Analysis for Teachers: Phonology, Lexis, Syntax

Course Description

Language is a regularly-patterned, meaning-making system. For teaching purposes, an understanding of the regularities, meanings, and underlying systems of language is an essential requirement in helping learners navigate the sometimes baffling data that they encounter.

This course explores the forms, meanings, and uses of English structure, and involves the description and analysis of the English sound system (phonology), the system of word formation (morphology), and sentence structure (syntax).

Course Outcomes

The ultimate purpose of language analysis is to enhance the effective teaching of English as a second language. By the end of the course, therefore, participants should:

- be familiar with the basic terms and concepts that are used to describe the phonological, morphological, and syntactic systems of the English language, insofar as they are relevant to the teaching of English
- be able to apply this knowledge to:
  - the identification and evaluation of the teaching objectives of instructional programs and materials
  - the formulation of appropriate learning objectives, and
  - to the analysis of learner language, including errors
- be equipped with the tools to continue their professional development in this field.

Figure 9.6 Course description and outcomes for an online course, Language Analysis for Teachers

The course has 10 units spread over 15 weeks. Most units run for 1 week and some for 2 weeks. Each unit has a specific number of lessons depending upon the natural breaks in each unit topic.

Look again at the course outcomes and compare it to the unit outcomes below. Note the introduction for the unit. What role does it play?

A Unit Introduction from an Online Course

Language Analysis for Teachers: Phonology, Lexis, Syntax

Unit 7—Lexis (2): The Meaning of Words

Introduction

This unit continues the theme of lexis (vocabulary) by moving from a focus on the form of words (covered in the previous unit) to a focus on the meaning of words. In this unit, we look at theories of word meaning (or semantics), including the view that word meaning is constructed out of basic elements of meaning, and the view that our understanding of a word's meaning is represented in the form of "best examples" (or prototypes). We then look at ways that words are interrelated so that their meanings are defined in relation to other words. Finally, we look at the way words gather associations through the way they are used in social and cultural contexts.

Key Concepts

lexicon	synonym	denotation
referent	antonym	connotation
componential analysis	hyponym	register
semantic features	metonym	style
prototype	lexical set	collocation

Learning Outcomes

By the end of this unit you should be able to:

- explain how words are said to "mean," and how concepts can be analyzed into their components;

- explain the role that prototypes play in assigning word meaning;

- describe the main ways in which word meaning is defined in relation to other words; and

- identify different ways that words are "colored" by their associations.

Unit 7 has four lessons:

1. The meaning of meaning

2. Features and prototypes (see pages 172–177)

Unit Introduction *(continued)*

3. Lexical relations

4. Associative meaning

Each of the above lessons contains readings, tasks, and assignments to complete. Please complete the lessons sequentially.

These are the main tasks you will be asked to do in this unit:

Discussion Board Tasks

- Compare differences between prototypical examples of different categories (not assessed).

- Evaluate the teacher's explanations of words (assessed).

- Discuss the validity of translating words from L2 to L1 (assessed).

Written Task

- Find a text and analyze its lexical content from three different points of view (assessed).

Figure 9.7
Language Analysis for Teachers, Unit 7 Introduction

Now look at the section-by-section outcomes of the unit in Figure 9.8. Again, compare them first with the Unit 7 outcomes and then the overall course outcomes. This is an excellent example of the anatomy of a well-constructed course.

Note: The outcome in black below is for the module you will be covering in the next chapter.

 Introductions and summaries are provided at the beginning and end of units.

 Learning outcomes are measurable and specific.

Note: While we set forth a set of standards in this book, we do not propose that all courses should be set up in exactly the same way. Scott Thornbury sets up a list of key concepts in the overview (see page 157). This will be particularly helpful to these students because one of Scott's books, *The A to Z of ELT*, an alphabetically listed collection of key ELT terms and concepts, is one of the texts for the course. Having the

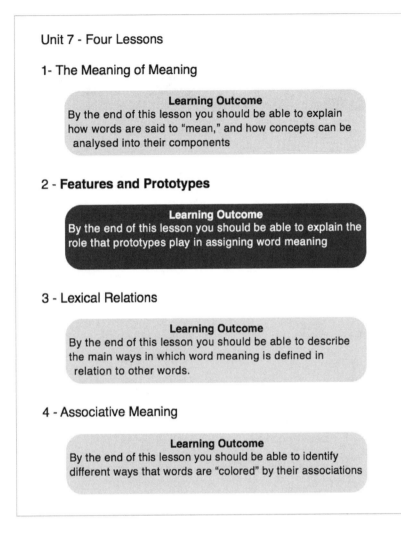

Figure 9.8 An online unit with four lessons and sets of learning outcomes

concepts ahead of time enables the students to prepare for the concepts covered in the unit.

Now, let's look at assessments. See Figure 9.9 for Scott Thornbury's outline of assessments in the syllabus.

Finally, let's look at the specific assignment from the syllabus. The students know exactly what to do, the assignments are explained in detail, and they know how much value each assignment has toward their grade.

 The website provides templates on each stage of this process.

Assessment

Course Requirement	Specifications	Words (approximately)	Value
1	Discussion board participation		30
2	8 assignments @ 5 points each	8 x 500 = 4000	35
3	2 longer assignments submitted at ends of weeks 8 and 12: 1500 words each	3000	35
	Total:	7000	100

Figure 9.9 An example of the course assessment section of the online syllabus

 All graded activities are listed upfront in the syllabus.

 The size of and due date for graded assignments are reasonable.

 Students can easily track their progress.

9.5 Summary and Standards

In this chapter, we have looked at the elements of an online course and its stages of development. We have paid special attention to the development of the learning outcomes and the online syllabus, including a detailed course outline. Once you have completed this foundation, you can move on to designing the lessons for the course.

☐ Learning outcomes are measurable and specific.

☐ The wording used to define learning outcomes is clear and definite.

☐ Course material is sufficient and directly related to learning outcomes.

- [ ] Resources and activities support learning outcomes.

- [ ] Assessments determine the degree to which the learners have achieved the required learning outcomes.

- [ ] Criteria/rubrics clearly inform learners as to how they will be assessed on specific assignments, such as online class participation.

- [ ] Contact information to advisors and technical help is provided in the syllabus.

- [ ] All graded activities are listed upfront in the syllabus.

- [ ] The manner of submission for graded assignments is clear.

- [ ] A syllabus including contact information, an outline, requirements, and guidelines is accessible from the start of the course and throughout.

- [ ] Instructions and requirements are stated simply, clearly, and logically.

- [ ] Consequences of missed deadlines and insufficient class participation are clearly stated and fair.

- [ ] The consequences of plagiarism, cheating, and failure to properly cite copyrighted material are emphasized.

- [ ] Content elements are presented in a logical sequence.

- [ ] Pedagogical steps build progressively, one upon the other, as is appropriate to the subject matter.

- [ ] Introductions and summaries are provided at the beginning and end of units.

- [ ] Learning outcomes are measurable and specific.

- [ ] All graded activities are listed upfront in the syllabus.

- [ ] The size of and due date for graded assignments are reasonable.

- [ ] Students can easily track their progress.

Chapter 10

Creating the Course Structure: Online Lessons

Let's now see how the material covered comes together in an online lesson. Terminology for online course design varies. We will begin by reviewing the terms we use and how we use them.

Unit structure

The lesson is the core learning component. Lessons may or may not be grouped into units. Typically, in a non-intensive class (e.g. 15 weeks), there may be 1 lesson per week or, perhaps, 1 lesson that lasts over 2 weeks. In an intensive class (i.e. the same class compressed into 6 weeks), there may be more than 1 lesson per week.

A lesson consists of one or more sections. The sections are broken down into segments. Segments in a section may consist of learning outcomes, an introduction, activities, a task-based video clip, etc. The lessons should follow the structure you have in place in your course outline in the syllabus.

10.1 What Replaces an Onsite Class Session?

Text-based lectures, whether in writing, audio, or video, are passive or receptive. To make the presentation of new knowledge productive or active, develop a varied series of activities so that the students interact with each other, the teacher, and the content. Have them analyze, combine, choose, create, collaborate, test themselves, explore, synthesize, reflect, etc.

There are many ways to create the kind of textured environment that keeps learners involved and interested. Use the following ideas to begin brainstorming:

- Rework the way materials are presented. Use different types of readings, and ask students to categorize, eliminate, question, add to, redesign, extend, etc. as is appropriate. Turn things on their heads. Provide solutions and have students figure out what the problem was (see Chapter 6).

- Incorporate varied media (see Chapter 7). The presentation of new knowledge and skills can come in many forms and combinations. Think of using, as is appropriate for the class you are designing: brief audio/video lectures, text/image-based slideshows, or written narratives. Multimedia learning can aid students in remembering and understanding the course content (Mayer, 2001). Use carefully chosen media resources joined to focused tasks to present new concepts.

- Change the presenters—alternate student or other voices with your own (see Chapter 7).

- Tap resources from different sources, including libraries, the internet, interviews, etc. (see Chapter 7).

- Use a mix of activities—incorporate collaborative activities (see Chapter 6).

- Provide frequent opportunities for reflection and self-assessment (see Chapter 8). Reflective activities, and self-assessment mixed in with activities, motivate the students by letting them know exactly where they are in the process.

We will walk you through an assortment of presentation examples and techniques. In an attempt to encourage you to create an engaging online learning environment in a rather straightforward way, we will limit our presentation options to the basics.

Let's review some standards that are particularly important at this point:

☑ Presentations of new knowledge and skills, activities, and assessments address a variety of learning styles.

☑ The manner of presenting new knowledge and skills is varied, including text, lists, organizational activities, reflective quizzes, readings, images, graphs, charts, etc.

☑ Presentations include examples, models, case studies, illustrations, etc. for clarification.

☑ Materials are authentic or relate to real-life applications.

☑ Topics and materials are up-to-date and relevant.

☑ Presentations include media and are varied.

☑ Activities engage students in higher-level thinking skills, including critical and creative thinking, analysis, and problem solving.

☑ Reflection and reflective activities come up throughout the course.

10.2   The First Lesson—Orienting Students

We will now look at some samples from featured teachers.

Collaboration Technologies
Week 1—Kristen Sosulski

The first is from Kristen Sosulski's course on Collaboration Technologies. We are showing you the lesson for the first week of class. Kristen is giving students a great deal of support for adjusting to the potentially new ways of communicating that they will encounter in her course. She provides clear instructions at every stage.

The material presented and worked through is broken down into a series of learning segments.

In the examples in this chapter, the teacher provides varied activities for the students to work through. Generally speaking, these may be many small activities that build upon one another in progressive steps, or larger activities, such as a group project, that have a series of steps within them. What is important is that students are involved with an array of activities that are interesting, challenging, and pedagogically sound.

Introduction

Welcome to Collaboration Technologies!

This is great course to take online since all the technologies that we'll be reviewing and using are web-based.

This course is offered in an intensive 6-week format. It's really important that you keep up with the course readings and honor the due dates for assignments and activities.

In this course we will explore possibilities afforded by and through various communication and collaborative technologies. Please review the syllabus carefully. The syllabus will provide you with an overview of the course content areas, requirements, required readings, and outline of assignments.

The bulk of the course content is available in the **Lessons** area of the course website. It includes all of the readings, course content, and assignments that are required from **Monday, June 28 through Sunday, July 4.**

A major goal for this first week is for the class to become oriented with the learning management system (LMS) in which you will be studying, communicating, and submitting your course assignments.

By the end of this lesson **you will be able to**:

- **understand** the importance of the collaborative process and factors that influence and shape the participants contributions in collaborative workspaces;

- **list** and **define** the six types of e-collaboration technologies;

- **apply** the electronic collaboration framework to your own academic and professional experience using collaborative technologies; and

- **identify** and **categorize** new e-collaboration technologies, and **reflect**, **describe**, and **share** your experiences using two types of e-collaboration tools.

Figure 10.1 Collaboration Technologies, Week 1, Lesson Introduction

Note: All examples in this chapter are presented in document format rather than screen format. While the same writing and visual design standards are followed, this is not exactly how these samples would look on a computer screen. We used this format for the sake of clarity. Screenshots are not as easy to read, and poorly designed LMSs are obscure at times.

Reflection

Read carefully through this example and the steps Kristen takes. Then reflect on which of the steps would be appropriate for your course.

Reading Assignment

During the early part of the week you are expected to review the syllabus for the course and *Emerging e-Collaboration Concepts and Applications*, Chapters 1 and 3. Details are below.

1. **Syllabus**. To learn about the course requirements please review the syllabus for this course.

Please note that the syllabus will be updated regularly, as readings and assignments may change based on your interests and areas of expertise. While the class has a set of assignments and readings defined, I like to customize the class based on student interest.

2. *Emerging e-Collaboration Concepts and Applications*, Chapters 1 and 3.

To begin learning about the different categories of collaboration technologies, read Chapters 1 and 3 from *Emerging e-Collaboration Concepts and Applications*. It covers key conceptual elements of e-collaboration.

Figure 10.2 Week 1, lesson readings

 See the website for a sample syllabus.

Activity: Introductions

Please introduce yourself and share something about yourself with the class. To do so, **reply** to the relevant **posting** in the **forums. Do not create a new topic.**

In your reply, tell us a little about yourself and what you hope to learn in this course, and how you think that knowledge will/can be applied in your career. Feel free to comment on the postings of your classmates by replying to their postings. At a minimum, read all the introductions of your classmates.

Due—6/30, 11:59 p.m., EST

Here's how you respond to a discussion in the **forum**:

* www.youtube.com/watch?v=Op2W3TljhKs&feature=player_embedded

Here's how you reply to a post in the **forum** by another class member:

* www.youtube.com/watch?v=wWCSLmHWLNs&feature=player_embedded

Figure 10.3 Week 1, social discussion activity

 Go to the website to see this section with live links.

 Activities lead to active interactions that involve course content and personal communication.

10.3 How to Present and Work Through New Knowledge and Skills Online

When designing a lesson, remember to begin with the learning outcomes for the week. The learning outcomes should be measurable and the content directly related to the learning outcomes. Decide what students will be doing to achieve the learning outcomes.

Set out a plan for staging the lessons. Will they begin the week with a reading or an activity? Then what? Identify where it is necessary for you to add explanations to support learning. How will you help them pace their learning? How will you assess learning?

Class Participation Assignment

Part 1

After completing the ice-breaker activities and the readings for week 1, go to the forum for week 1 and respond to the following:

Reflect on your own experience using collaborative technologies. Specifically, provide two examples of e-collaboration technologies that you have used in the past. Define the following:

1. Name of the e-collaborative technology.

2. Describe the collaborative task.

3. Describe the participants in the collaborative task.

4. Describe the physical environment of the participants.

5. Describe the social environment of the participants.

Due—7/2, 11:59 p.m. EST

Part 2

Next, between 7/2 and 7/4 respond to your assigned partner's posting by categorizing the technology that they described in Chapter 3. Provide two other examples of technologies that fall into the same category.

Due—7/4, 11:59 p.m. EST

Figure 10.4 Week 1, topical discussion activity

Note: Pairs should be assigned here once the course begins.

 Course material is sufficient and directly related to learning outcomes.

 Learning outcomes are measurable and specific.

Breaking up Material into Chunks or Subtopics

The area where teachers present new material in an LMS is still sometimes called a lecture. This is a holdover from the onsite classroom or the early days of online, when teachers posted a class-length audio or video version of an onsite lecture. More typically, teachers would turn class lectures into text and post them online.

Posting long lecture notes or a long video of a lecture online is not the most effective way to present new information to students. We have learned with time and research that students find such unbroken density in content very difficult to deal with online.

At the most basic level, online content must be broken up. You may have heard this referred to as "chunking." Chunking does not just mean that you break up text into shorter paragraphs. It means that the presentation is broken down into a series of mini-presentations.

☑ Blocks of information are broken up or "chunked" into incremental learning sections, segments, or steps as is appropriate to the subject matter.

Use of Text and Images

Learners can better understand an explanation when it is presented in words and pictures than when it is presented in words only.

Mayer (2001: 1)

A great deal of variety can be achieved by using a mix of different text-based segments, including activities, short readings, text-based supplementary materials from the internet, and reflective self-assessments. Such a mix keeps things flowing and offers opportunities to develop a range of thinking skills.

In the best cases, mini-lectures are varied in design and presentation as well. Depending upon the content area, charts, photos, illustrations, links, and audio and video are used to create a textured, multi-facteted environment. The purposeful development of content in different ways, and from different perspectives, clarifies and extends understanding.

However, when used gratuitously (i.e. variety for the sake of variety), it can distract and even detract. For example, presenting text slides along with narration interferes with understanding. This type of simultaneous redundancy impedes learning (Mayer, 2001). It is best to keep things both varied and simple at the same time.

Be open to new ways of communication that cut down on your dependency on text as the sole means of presenting information. If you are comfortable with speaking, for example, include some brief audio or video clips of you explaining or demonstrating something.

☑ Courses include a variety of relevant multimedia to support learning (e.g. audio, video, recommended podcasts, illustrations, photographs, charts, and graphs).

☑ Content is designed simply and clearly to avoid information overload (e.g. avoid narrating while written text is visible, using distracting images for decoration, presenting too much information at once, etc.).

☑ Details in images, graphs, charts, and diagrams are easy to see.

10.4   A Later Lesson: Introducing or Reinforcing New Knowledge

Language Analysis
Lesson 7, Section 2—Scott Thornbury

Now that you have seen an example of a class setup lesson, let's move to a lesson that is further inside a course.

Depending upon the part played by assigned readings, the presentation may be introducing or reinforcing the new knowledge. In the following lesson Scott Thornbury is doing the former.

In general, it is more common and more pedagogically sound for skills-based lessons to be broken down into subtopics and multiple sections. Skills-based knowledge is usually presented in small steps that build upon each other.

For liberal arts, courses such as theory and philosophy, or literature, it may be more common to have only one or two sections in a lesson.

The point is that the material presented and worked through is broken down into a series of learning segments.

In both samples in this chapter the teacher provides varied activities for the student to work through. These may be many small activities that build upon one another in progressive steps, or larger activities, such as a group project, that have a series of steps within them. What is important is that students are involved with an array of activities and tasks that are interesting, challenging, and pedagogically sound.

The sample we are looking at here is the second section in a unit on semantics.

Reflection

We will approach this review of Scott Thornbury's class as a "mega reflective activity" of sorts. At this point we have covered the basic components and gone through the standards for presenting new knowledge and skills. Let's examine what we know through this example.

As we go through the lesson, we will periodically pose questions. Why we are asking the questions may be obvious. Our point is to have you reflect on how these points have been dealt with in an online environment.

We suggest that you go through this lesson twice.

1. Go through the lesson imagining that you are the student. Do not read the questions that appear in between the boxed sections of the lesson. Instead think about these:
   - Was the writing clear?
   - Were the pictures helpful?
   - Were the things you were asked to do helpful?
   - Imagine if this were all text with no visuals and no tasks/activities. What would that have been like?

2. Now read the questions posed between the sections. These will help you analyze the module as a teacher.

Let's first see some details from the first section in lesson 7, "The Meaning of Meaning." Here's the outcome:

> By the end of this section you should be able to explain how words are said to "mean," and how concepts can be analyzed into their components.

One of the concepts introduced here is componential analysis:

> Theorists have attempted to break down concepts into "atoms" of meaning, using what is called "componential analysis." The underlying principle of componential analysis is that all words can be analyzed using a finite set of components.

Now look at the same items for the second section (Figure 10.5).

What does the learning outcome tell you and how is that helpful?

What is covered in the short introductory statement? 1... 2... 3...

---

2. Features and prototypes

Learning Outcome
By the end of this section you should be able to explain the role that prototypes play in assigning word meaning.

In the previous section we saw how componential analysis attempts to explain how the meaning of a word is composed, or constructed, from simpler meanings. However, the quest for the definitive semantic features of a concept, even a concept as simple as table, is not easy. How can we be sure that we have only those features that are common to all tables? Here, for example, is a componential analysis of the word chair:

chair (object), (physical), (non-living), (artifact), (furniture), (portable), (something with legs), (something with a back), (something with a seat), (seat for one)

Figure 10.5

What three things is Scott asking students to do in task 7.2.1 in Figure 10.6?

Is there a progression from one section to the next?

Think of Bloom's hierarchy (see Appendix A). What level of thinking skills are being dealt with here?

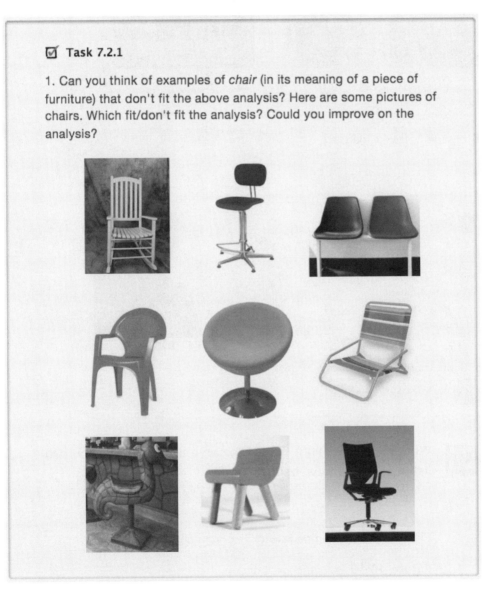

☑ **Task 7.2.1**

1. Can you think of examples of *chair* (in its meaning of a piece of furniture) that don't fit the above analysis? Here are some pictures of chairs. Which fit/don't fit the analysis? Could you improve on the analysis?

Figure 10.6 Lesson 2, task 1, part 1

How does the second part of this task in Figure 10.7 (differ from the first? Is there a progression?

2. Attempt to analyze the concept of table in the same way. Here are some pictures of tables that might help:

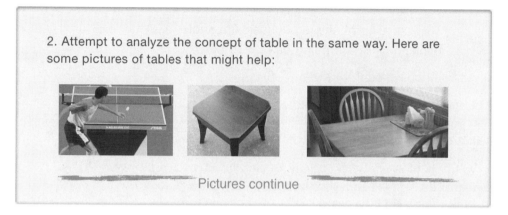

Pictures continue

Figure 10.7 Lesson 2, task 1, part 2

Audio

Click the speaker
icon for my analysis
of the task.

Figure 10.8 Scott Thornbury discusses the task in Figure 10.6

The New School/Matthew Sussman

 What purposes might the audio serve at this point? You can listen to it on the website.

Figure 10.9 (facing page, top) Text from course

Figure 10.10 (facing page, bottom)

The difficulty in identifying the necessary and sufficient "atoms" of meaning that are common to all members of such broad categories as, say, chairs or tables, has led some theorists to question the view that word meanings are the combination of a finite number of semantic features. Moreover, word meanings are often quite "fuzzy" at the edges, with the meaning of one word "leaking" into the meaning of different, but related, words. In one famous experiment, the sociolinguist Labov asked informants to name various containers.

> "They not only disagreed with one another over bowls, cups and vases, but were inconsistent from day to day. Certain shapes were clear in instances of particular containers, but others varied: something might be a bowl when full of potatoes, but a vase when it held flowers." (Aitchison, 1997: 65).

☑ **Task 7.2.2 Self Assessment**

Test yourself: which of the following would you classify as a cup, mug, bowl, or vase (or none of the above!)?

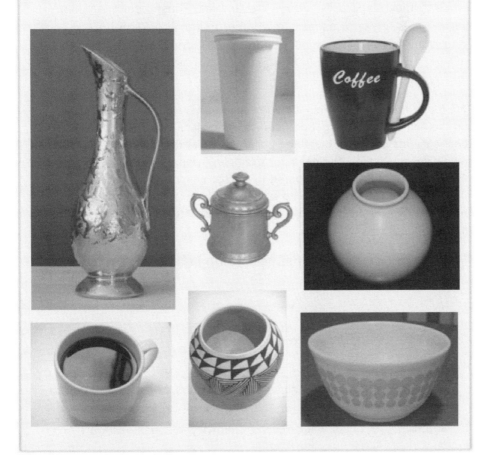

What simple yet critical piece of information is added in the short statement in Figure 10.9?

What purpose does this self-assessment serve? (See Figure 10.10.)

Read the text selection below (in Figure 10.11).

At this point think about what the student has learned.

Note: Notice the marks around the term **Prototype theory**. These indicate that this is one of the key concepts covered in the introduction.

From the above activity, it should be clear that we don't rank all examples of a category as being equally representative. Some examples are more "typical" than others. <**Prototype theory**> argues that we understand the meaning of a word by reference to these typical—or "best"—examples. These best examples are used by the mind as a way of assessing whether marginal or doubtful examples belong to the same category. As Schmitt (2000) points out, our notion of what might be a best example of a category is partly culturally determined:

> Rosch (1975) found that people within a culture tend to have a relatively uniform idea of what the best examples are. For instance, Americans considered robins to be the best example of a bird, because robins represent the attributes people most commonly associate with birdiness: for example, flying, laying eggs, building nests, and singing. When compared to robins, penguins and ostriches had enough of these 'birdy' features to be considered birds, although not typical ones. Although bats fly, they did not have enough other features to be considered birds (p. 25).

Figure 10.11

How has the topic evolved from task 7.2.1 to 7.2.3 (Figures 10.6 to 10.12)?

This is an international class with members from many different locations around the globe. How engaged do you imagine an international class will be in the following discussion board activity?

☑ **Task 7.2.3   Discussion**

What - to you - is the "best example" of the following categories? How might your choice differ from that of a person from another culture that you are familiar with?

1. flower
2. vegetable
3. vehicle
4. dwelling
5. sport
6. woman's clothing
7. musical instrument
8. profession

Link to Discussion Board Task 7.2.3

Use this link to post your response. Post your response on the Discussion thread "Prototypes", and read and respond to the postings of your colleagues. (This task is not assessed).

Link to Next Section

Figure 10.12 A topical discussion activity

Here are some of the qualities you might have noticed in this lesson:

- The learning outcomes clearly describe the purpose of the lesson.

- Scott has broken up, or chunked, the lesson into a series of sections designed to keep the students moving forward, step by step, and engaged.

- His course narrative is brief.

- His tone throughout is casual without being colloquial. While he uses British English, and is a native of New Zealand, he uses English that can be understood across a range of varieties of English.

- Although the layout here is not the same as that in an actual online class, the use of space is similar. The images in this presentation break up the space and provide white space. When introducing challenging content, such space helps to clarify. As John Maeda points out: "The opportunity lost by increasing the amount of blank space is gained back with enhanced attention to what remains" (Maeda, 2006: 56).

Reflection

Review the work of all three featured teachers: Joelle Scally (Chapter 2), Kristen Sosulski (Chapter 10), and Scott Thornbury (Chapter 10) in terms of the checklist of standards at the end of this chapter.

 All three modules are available for viewing on the website, in selection 10.4. The best way to proceed with this exercise is to view the modules on the website while you go through the standards.

10.5 DIY—Do it Yourself

Following are a variety of lists, charts, and suggestions for you to refer to when working through a lesson. Use all or only those that best suit you.

Let's look again at the segments in a lesson:

- Outcome
- Introduction
- Activity
- Activity
- Activity
- ...
- Summary.

 A template for designing lessons can be downloaded from the website. It is based on the following:

1. Decide how many sections you need to cover the topic of your lesson. Remember, skills-based courses usually need

to be broken up into small steps that build upon one another. Consequently you may need to group them into a few sections/subtopics.

Once you have defined the topic or subtopic for a section a the next two steps are straightforward:

2. Write the learning outcome(s).

3. Write the introduction.

4. Analyze and break up your content into a series of "chunks" that make sense.

5. Review the material and see where or how it might be enhanced by images, charts, graphs, etc. Can any of the chunks of information be transformed into or supported by audio or video? Would linking to a resource expand the content in a meaningful way?

A checklist of images, multimedia, and linked resources, including all items covered in Chapter 7, can be downloaded from the website.

W **A more extensive checklist can be downloaded from the website.**

For now, look over this list for activity ideas:

- Activities such as practice exercises, discussion board, tasks, etc. (see Chapter 6). Which?

- Assigned readings with guidelines. What kinds of guidelines might you set up to make readings more interactive and challenging?

- Assigned research-based student presentation segments. Where is the research done? What do students do with the results? Do they present them as is, or transform or combine them in some way? Do they do these alone or in collaboration with other class members? Who and how many others?

- Periodic self-assessments and reflective activities. How often?

- Guest speakers. Who? Why? How? Relationship to topic? Who provides feedback?

- Experiences from the field. Who? What? How? In what form? Primary or secondary? What is the feedback? Who provides it?

- Assigned reports on real-life research such as surveys and interviews.

- Brief audio and video clips (2–5 minutes). Ready-made, teacher-made, or student-made?

- Student presentations. Individuals or groups?

Tip

For those of you who are new to teaching online, don't try to do it all at once. Focus on a limited set of techniques the first time out. See what works for you. Then you can enhance the work you have done and adjust the course each time you teach it, if you need to.

10.6 Summary and Standards

At this point you have all you need to create engaging, pedagogically sound online presentations, lessons, resources, activities, and syllabus. The basic principles have been covered. The exercise of comparing the example lessons to the entire list of standards should have set the standards in your mind.

This is the end of the online course design process. When your course goes live, this is where the teaching begins. During this time you'll be making weekly announcements, participating and monitoring online discussions, providing feedback on course assignments and activities, structuring group activities (such as putting students into teams—something that cannot be done prior to the class beginning), asking your students for feedback on the course design, pace, and structure, and, finally, communicating with students regularly to ensure a well-engaged online classroom. References will be provided on the website to resources that can guide you in your online teaching.

☐ Presentations of new knowledge and skills, activities, and assessments address a variety of learning styles.

☐ The manner of presenting new knowledge and skills is varied, including text, lists, organizational activities, reflective quizzes, readings, images, graphs, charts, etc.

☐ Presentations include examples, models, case studies, illustrations, etc. for clarification.

☐ Materials are authentic or relate to real-life applications.

☐ Topics and materials are up-to-date and relevant.

☐ Presentations include media and are varied.

☐ Activities engage students in higher-level thinking skills, including critical and creative thinking, analysis, and problem solving.

☐ Reflection and reflective activities come up throughout the course.

☐ Activities lead to active interactions that involve course content and personal communication.

☐ Blocks of information are broken up or "chunked" into incremental learning sections, segments, or steps as is appropriate to the subject matter.

☐ Courses include a variety of relevant multimedia to support learning (e.g. audio, video, recommended podcasts, illustrations, photographs, charts, and graphs).

☐ Content is designed simply and clearly to avoid information overload (e.g. avoid narrating while written text is visible, using distracting images for decoration, presenting too much information at once, etc.).

☐ Details in images, graphs, charts, and diagrams are easy to see.

Appendix A Writing Learning Outcomes

A.1 Learning Outcomes Support Online Course Development

Used deliberately and carefully, learning outcomes become powerful tools for defining the development of an online learning module.

The care you put into the thoughtful writing of and follow-through on learning outcomes is key to assuring that the online course matches the onsite equivalent in content and challenge.

Outcomes keep programs and courses on track.
Programs intended to be practical professional preparation, for example, may devote too much time to theory and not enough to applied practice. Outcomes can keep the practical in sight.

In skills-based courses, such as math and languages, outcomes can assure that learners move smoothly through levels of acquisition and expertise.

While there is some debate on the use of outcomes in the humanities, they can and should be used. Here also, learning outcomes assure learners that they have acquired the skills, knowledge, and an understanding of thinking processes involved in analysis, evaluation, and creation.

Outcomes motivate. Because online study is more flexible than onsite, it appeals to special segments of the population that need to fit study into their busy schedule. Most cannot afford to waste money, time, or energy. Outcomes provide clearly communicated expectations for what a course will enable them to do. As such, outcomes can reassure and motivate learners. Furthermore, they enable learners to evaluate their course.

A.2 Outcomes vs. Objectives

The terms "outcomes" and "objectives" are often used interchangeably. However, there is an implied difference in the two. **Objectives** outline goals for the teacher to reach in a learning segment. They are **teacher-focused**.

Outcomes speak of a change in the learner. Learning outcomes are stated in terms of what the learner will know or be able to do if he has successfully completed a unit. As such, they are **learner-centered**.

Expressing goals in outcomes is very motivating for the learner. For example, assume that this guide is being used in a staff development training group. One outcome would be **"You will be able to identify and provide examples of the standards and techniques used to design effective online courses."** This tells you that you are acquiring knowledge and skills that will get you to your goal (provided that you meet the requirements set out).

Universities and schools increasingly require that academic achievement be determined in terms of learning outcomes. It is terrific public relations for a teacher, trainer, program, or institution to declare that they can provide a specific set of skills and/or a specific level of academic achievement for their learners. This provides a check on the program. Educational institutions and companies that deliver on their promises graduate learners of a quality that fully supports their success in their chosen field or profession.

The three most challenging steps when devising and using learning outcomes are:

- writing them;

- assuring that you have provided all the course material and activities needed for achieving them; and

- assessing that the outcomes have been achieved.

A.3 Rationales for Writing Learning Outcomes

A learning outcome states what the learner will know or be able to do at the end of a learning unit. The unit may be a segment, module, or even the course itself.

Well-written learning outcomes:

- are specific;

- are clearly and concisely written;

- clarify for learners why they are doing what they are doing;

- support and help to provide a framework for the online development process by:
    - defining the knowledge and/or skills to be acquired;
    - helping to determine the content and activities for the course by pointing to the kinds of thinking skills needed; and
    - providing goals for assessment;

- help to insure the quality of the course; and

- set up an agreement between teacher and learner as to their relative responsibilities.

A.4 How to Write Clear, Concise Learning Outcomes

The first step is to focus on the verbs used in learning outcomes. This may sound very straightforward but, in fact, the classification of levels of thinking directly informs the choice of verbs. So, let's start there.

Classifying Levels of Thinking

Benjamin Bloom classified the order of the development of higher thinking skills. Bloom's *Taxonomy of Educational Objectives* (1956) has been used to describe the progressive development of higher-ordered thinking skills for more than 50 years.

Here's how it works. At the first level (the bottom of Figure A.1), the learner knows about or remembers a concept. Now she can move to the next step: understanding the concept. Next, she can work on applying what she understands.

About 20 years ago, a student of Bloom's, Lorin Anderson, revised the taxonomy using verb forms instead of nouns to explain the process. Also, the top two categories were revised. This revised approach is on the right column of Figure A.1.

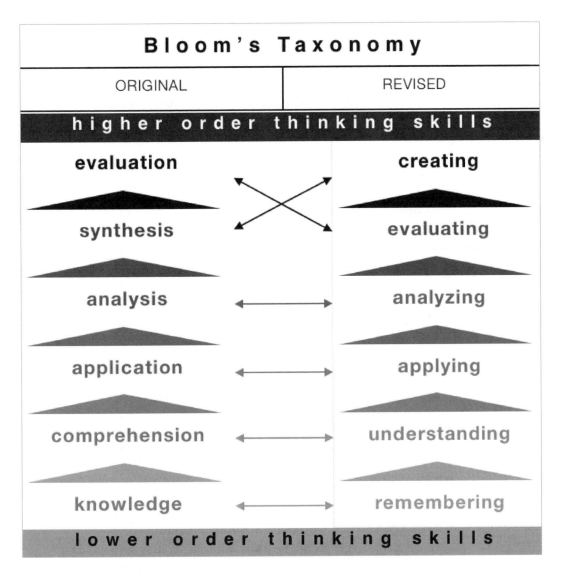

Figure A.1 Bloom's Taxonomy

Using Active Verbs

Because outcomes usually describe something the learner will be able to do, they are described using active verbs. For example, specific active verbs such as "match," "locate," or "describe" would be used instead of "understand." Each order of thinking skills has certain measurable active verbs associated with it. Figure A.2 provides some examples.

Thinking skills	active, specific verbs
creating	Plan, assemble, construct, develop, design, create.....
evaluating	Appraise, judge, edit, rate, debate, estimate, interpret...
analyzing	Differentiate, classify, infer, categorize, analyze, calculate, contrast, compare....
applying	Demonstrate, modify, prepare, produce, show, paint, use, sketch, illustrate, teach...
understanding	Estimate, explain, give examples, paraphrase, explain why, summarize, recognize.
remembering	Describe, identify, list, name, outline, select, match.

Figure A.2 The active verbs associated with the revised Bloom's taxonomy

Three Components—Behavior, Conditions, Measurable Criteria

The most common way to begin writing a learning outcome is by stating "You will be able to..." thus indicating a change, or acquisition of skills or behavior on the part of the learner. The challenge is to be sure that what follows this phrase is definite and the verb is active.

Learning outcomes include these two components:

- **Behavior**. What will the learner be able to do?

- **Conditions**. How will the learner be able to do it?

However, a third component is implied:

- **Measurable criteria**. How well will the learner be able to do it? Or, what is the minimum level of achievement acceptable to deem learner performance acceptable for achieving the outcome?

Clearly, if the student does not do her part in the learning process, she will not end up "being able to do" what is laid out in the learning outcome. Her grade indicates the extent to which she has achieved the learning or acquisition set out.

Figure A.3 below sets up a format for writing learning outcomes. The measurable criteria are assured by using verbs that indicate a measurable aspect of learning.

Notice that Figure A.3 contains the two core components of a learning outcome. How measurable criteria is determined will be covered in the evaluation plan syllabus.

behavior	conditions	measurable criteria
explain how......	in a 10 minute video presentation	*see syllabus*
describe the process......	in a paper, no more than 200 words	*see syllabus*
show how......	in a three page report	*see syllabus*
outline	In a lesson plan	*see syllabus*
analyze.....	in writing on discussion forum	*see syllabus*

Figure A.3 Components of a learning outcome

Well-written learning outcomes act as a guide and double check for the following standards:

 Learning outcomes are measurable and specific.

 The wording used to define learning outcomes is clear and definite.

A.5 Resources

- "Bloom's *Taxonomy*—Bloom's Digital Taxonomy": www.techlearning.com/techlearning/archives/2008/04/AndrewChurches.pdf

- "Writing Learning Outcomes—Oxford Brooks University" (some suggestions): www.brookes.ac.uk/services/ocsd/2_learntch/writing_learning_outcomes.html

- Self-correcting quiz on Bloom's *Taxonomy*: http://school.discoveryeducation.com/quizzes22/honglin/LearningOutcomes.html

Appendix B   Using the Standards Checklist

Standards encourage consistency, clear learner expectations, and overall quality and design principles across the program. This list also serves as a standards index. Each standard is followed by the page number(s) it appears on within the chapters.

B.1   Learning Outcomes

☐ 1. Learning outcomes for an online course are identical to those of the onsite version. **23**

☐ 2. Learning outcomes are measurable and specific. **146, 158, 168**

☐ 3. Course material is sufficient and directly related to learning outcomes. **23, 146, 168**

☐ 4. Resources and activities support learning outcomes. **80, 146**

☐ 5. Assessments determine the degree to which the learners have achieved the required learning outcomes. **130, 146**

B.2   Ease of Communication

☐ 1. The writing style is clear, concise, and direct. **43**

☐ 2. Sentences and paragraphs are brief and to the point. **43**

☐ 3. Familiar or common words are used when possible. **45**

☐ 4. Jargon, clichés, and colloquial and idiomatic expressions are avoided. **45**

☐ 5. The meaning of special terms, abbreviations, and acronyms is easy to access. **46**

☐ 6. Labeling in all presentation materials is accurate, readable, and clear. **47, 118**

☐ 7. The wording used to define learning outcomes is clear and definite. **146**

☐ 8. Instructions and requirements are stated simply, clearly, and logically. **48, 154**

☐ 9. A supportive second-person conversational tone is used throughout the course. **46**

☐ 10.The course material has been edited for language and grammar. **49**

B.3   Pedagogical and Organizational Design

☐ 1. A syllabus including contact information, an outline, requirements, and guidelines is accessible from the start of the course and throughout. **154**

☐ 2. Introductions and summaries are provided at the beginning and end of units. **158**

☐ 3. Blocks of information are broken up or "chunked" into incremental learning sections, segments, or steps as is appropriate to the subject matter. **169**

☐ 4. Content elements are presented in a logical sequence. **155**

☐ 5. Pedagogical steps build progressively, one upon the other, as is appropriate to the subject matter. **155**

☐ 6. Numbers are used to identify sequential steps in a task or process. They are also used for rankings and setting priorities. **61**

☐ 7. Bullets are used to highlight a series of items that are not prioritized or sequential. **61**

B.4 Visual Design

☐ 1. Page layout is uncluttered and open, and includes a significant amount of white space. **54**

☐ 2. There is sufficient space between lines, paragraphs, and to the right and left of text so that it stands out and is easy to read. **54**

☐ 3. Text is left-justified and right margins are ragged. **55**

☐ 4. Headings and subheadings are used consistently to logically organize content. **56**

☐ 5. A universal sans serif web typeface (e.g. Verdana) assures access across platforms and enhances screen readability. **57**

☐ 6. Type size should be large enough to be easily readable by all students. **57**

☐ 7. Bold and italic typefaces are used sparingly only to emphasize important items. **58**

☐ 8. Underlining is used only for hyperlinks. **58**

☐ 9. Words in all caps are avoided. **58**

☐ 10.Use bullets or numbers to set apart items that can be listed. **61**

☐ 11.Color is used with purpose. **60**

☐ 12.There is good contrast between text and background. **60**

☐ 13.Visual elements (e.g. icons, shading, and color) are used consistently to distinguish between different types of course elements (e.g. lessons, assignments, audio, and video). **61**

☐ 14.Details in images, graphs, charts, and diagrams are easy to see. **118, 170**

☐ 15.Content is designed simply and clearly to avoid information overload (e.g. avoid narrating while written text is visible, using distracting images for decoration, presenting too much information at once, etc.). **170**

B.5   Engaged Learning

☐ 1. Activities encourage active interactions that involve course content and personal communication. **80**

☐ 2. Presentations of new knowledge and skills, activities, and assessments address a variety of learning styles. **72, 126, 163**

☐ 3. Presentations include examples, models, case studies, illustrations, etc. for clarification. **164**

☐ 4. Materials are authentic or relate to real-life applications. **126, 164**

☐ 5. The manner of presenting new knowledge and skills is varied, including text, lists, organizational activities, reflective quizzes, readings, images, graphs, charts, etc. **163**

☐ 6. Courses include a variety of relevant multimedia to support learning (e.g. audio, video, recommended podcasts, illustrations, photographs, charts, and graphs). **114, 170**

☐ 7. Presentations include media and are varied. **164**

☐ 8. Activities are frequent and varied. Students may respond to questions, select options, provide information, or interact with others. **80**

☐ 9. Activities engage students in higher-level thinking skills, including critical and creative thinking, analysis, and problem solving. **80, 164**

☐ 10. Topics and materials are up-to-date and relevant. **126, 164**

☐ 11. Reflection and reflective activities come up throughout the course. **164**

☐ 12. Bibliographies and reference lists include a variety of resources, including web links, books, journals, video, and downloadable text and audio files as is appropriate. **127**

B.6 **Collaboration and Community**

- ☐ 1. Activities lead to active interactions that involve course content and personal communication. **167**

- ☐ 2. There are sufficient opportunities for learners to work collaboratively. **76, 105**

- ☐ 3. Learners take responsibility for their learning and, at times, the learning of others. **73**

- ☐ 4. The teacher is a participant in the learning process. **73**

- ☐ 5. Learners are encouraged to interact with others (fellow classmates, course guests, etc.) and benefit from their experience and expertise. **78, 105, 122**

- ☐ 6. Class participation activities (e.g. discussion boards, wikis, social networks) are used to encourage collaboration. **75**

- ☐ 7. Procedures for group activities are specified so that students are aware of their role and responsibility in collaborative activities. **78, 105**

- ☐ 8. Collaborative activities are designed to facilitate a safe learning environment. **78**

- ☐ 9. An online space (e.g. discussion board, social network) is in place for students to meet outside the class. **85**

- ☐ 10. Students are encouraged to share resources as is appropriate. **78**

B.7 **Assessment**

- ☐ 1. The relationship between learning outcomes and assessments is evident. **130**

- ☐ 2. Course includes ongoing and frequent assessment. **131**

- ☐ 3. Graded elements are clearly distinguished from those that are ungraded. **134**

- ☐ 4. Graded assignments are varied (e.g. special projects, reflective assignments, research papers, case studies, presentations, group work, etc.). **131**

☐ 6. Students are given clear expectations and criteria for assignments. Examples are included for clarification when needed. **136**

☐ 7. Criteria/rubrics clearly inform learners as to how they will be assessed on specific assignments, such as online class participation. **139, 150**

☐ 8. Grading criteria are outlined in the course syllabus and within the assignment or activity itself. **136**

☐ 9. Criteria and procedures for peer review and evaluation are clear. **133**

B.8 Feedback

☐ 1. Teacher, peer-to-peer, guest, and automated feedback clarifies, amplifies, and extends the topic. **126, 133**

☐ 2. Teacher feedback is provided in a timely fashion. **131**

☐ 3. Students know when and how they will receive feedback from instructors. **134**

☐ 4. Self-correcting and self-assessment activities are used throughout the course to enable learners to vary the pace of their learning as is appropriate to the subject matter. **133, 142**

B.9 Evaluation and Grading

☐ 1. All graded activities are listed upfront in the syllabus. **151, 160**

☐ 2. The size of and due date for graded assignments are reasonable. **130, 160**

☐ 3. The manner of submission for graded assignments is clear. **151**

☐ 4. The relationship between graded elements and the final grade is clear. **134**

☐ 5. Consequences of missed deadlines and insufficient class participation are clearly stated and fair. **154**

☐ 6. Class participation/ discussion should account for 15–30 percent of the final grade. **139**

☐ 7. Students can easily track their progress. **136, 160**

☐ 8. The consequences of plagiarism, cheating, and failure to properly cite copyrighted material are emphasized. **113, 154**

B.10 Ease of Access

☐ 1. Direct links are provided to course materials and resources.

☐ 2. Links are working and correct.

☐ 3. Resource material is accessible to all students in commonly used formats. **113**

☐ 4. The format of multimedia should be specified, with a direct link to a required plug-in when necessary. **119**

☐ 5. Audio and video material appearing within a lesson should be brief. **120**

☐ 6. When possible, course material is portable (e.g. text can be downloaded or printed out, material is transferable to other devices, and presentations can be downloaded, printed out, or saved). **127**

☐ 7. Contact information to advisors and technical help is provided in the syllabus. **150**

☐ 8. Cross-referencing and links to items in other parts of the course are provided. **127**

Note: All of the above items must be carefully considered when teaching online on an international level because internet connections and speeds may vary from area to area.

References

ALTEC (2008) "Rubistar: What Is a Rubric?," available at: http://rubistar.4teachers.org/index.php?screen=WhatIs&module=Rubistar (accessed September 7, 2010).

Bloom, B.S. (Ed.) (1956) *Taxonomy of Educational Objectives: The Classification of Educational Goals. Handbook I: Cognitive Domain*, New York: Longman.

Boulton, M. (2007) "Whitespace," available at: www.alistapart.com/articles/whitespace/ (accessed April 21, 2010).

Brown, T. (2003) "Screen Typefaces," available at: http://adminstaff.vassar.edu/tibrown/thesis/screenfaces.html (accessed April 21, 2010).

Chickering, A.W. & Gamson, Z.F. (1987) "Seven Principles for Good Practice in Undergraduate Education," *The American Association for Higher Education Bulletin*, March.

Conrad, R. & Donaldson, J. (2004) *Engaging the Online Learner*, San Francisco, CA: Jossey-Bass.

Dewey, J. (1997 [1938]) *Experience and Education*, New York: Free Press.

Educause (2010) "Seven Things You Should Know About Assessing Online Team-based Learning," available at: www.educause.edu/ELI/ELIResources/7ThingsYouShouldKnowAboutAsses/210831 (accessed September 7, 2010).

Edutopia (1997) "Big Thinkers: Howard Gardner on Multiple Intelligences," available at: www.edutopia.org/multiple-intelligences-howard-gardner-video (accessed April 15, 2010).

Gardner, H. (1993) *Frames of Mind: The Theory of Multiple Intelligences*, New York: Basic Books.

Horton, S. (2005) *Access by Design: A Guide to Universal Usability for Web Designers*, Upper Saddle River, NJ: New Riders Press.

Horton, S. (2006) "Design Simply. Universal Usability: A Universal Design Approach to Web Usability," available at: www.universalusability.com/access_by_design/fundamentals/simply.html (accessed April 21, 2010).

Lamb, B. (2004) "Wide Open Spaces: Wikis Ready or Not," *EDUCAUSE Review*, September–October: 36–48.

Lidwell, W., Holden, K., & Butler, J. (2003) *Universal Principles of Design: 125 Ways to Influence Perception, Increase Appeal, Make Better Design Decisions, and Teach Through Design*, Beverly, MA: Rockport Publishers.

Lynch, P.J. & Horton, S. (2009) *Web Style Guide*, 3rd Edition, New Haven, CT: Yale University Press, available at: http://webstyleguide.com (accessed May 3, 2010).

References

Madden, D. (1999) "17 Elements of Good Online Courses," available at: http://honolulu.hawaii.edu/intranet/committees/FacDevCom/guidebk/online/web-elem.htm (accessed January 6, 2010).

Maeda, J. (2006) *Laws of Simplicity*, Cambridge, MA: MIT Press.

Mayer, R.E. (2001) *Multimedia Learning*, New York: Cambridge University Press.

Mayer, R.E. (2005) *The Cambridge Handbook of Multimedia Learning*, New York: Cambridge University Press.

Motive (2008) "Motive Guides: Web Typography," available at: www.motive.co.nz/guides/typography/webfonts.php (accessed April 21, 2010).

New York University School of Continuing and Professional Studies (2010) "Introduction to Macroeconomics," available at: http://content.scps.nyu.edu/course (accessed September 7, 2010).

Orwell, G. (1946) *Politics and the English Language*, London: Horizon.

Palloff, R.M. & Pratt, K. (2005) *Collaborating Online: Learning Together in Community*, San Francisco, CA: Jossey-Bass.

Palloff, R.M. & Pratt, K. (2007) *Building Online Learning Communities*, San Francisco, CA: Jossey-Bass.

Prensky, M. (2001) "Digital Natives, Digital Immigrants," available at: www.marcprensky.com/writing/Prensky%20-%20Digital%20Natives,%20Digital%20Immigrants%20-%20Part1.pdf (accessed April 21, 2010).

Quality Matters (2006) "Inter-institutional Quality Assurance in Online Learning," available at: http://qualitymatters.org.

Reeves, T. (2006) "How Do You Know They Are Learning? The Importance of Alignment in Higher Education," *International Journal of Learning Technology*, 2(4): 294–309.

Salmon, G. (2002) *eTivities: The Key to Active Online Learning*. New York: RoutledgeFalmer.

Shaul, M. (2007) "Assessing Online Discussion Forum Participation," *International Journal of Information and Communication Technology Education*, 3: 39–46.

Strunk, Jr., W. (1918) *The Elements of Style*, Ithaca, NY: W.P. Humphrey.

U.S. Department of Education, Office of Planning, Evaluation, and Policy Development (2009) *Evaluation of Evidence-based Practices in Online Learning: A Meta-analysis and Review Of Online Learning Studies*, Washington, DC: U.S. Department of Education.

Watrall, E. (2010) "Developing an Electronic Communication Policy," available at: http://chronicle.com/blogPost/Developing-an-Electronic/23606/sid=wc&utm_source=wc&utm_medium=en (accessed April 30, 2010).

Zeinstejer, R. (2008) "The Wiki Revolution: A Challenge to Traditional Education," *TESL-EJ*, 4: 1–8.